SHEILA CHURCH-MCSWEEN

DEVOTIONAL
WORKBOOK

Reflections of
A Spiritual Awakening

SHEILA JEANS PUBLISHING, LLC

Reflections of a Spiritual Awakening
Devotional Workbook
All Rights Reserved.
Copyright © 2012 Sheila Church-McSween
V2.0

Cover Photo © 2012 JupiterImages Corporation. All rights reserved - used with permission.

Sheila Jeans Publishing, LLC
Detroit, Michigan
www.sheilajeanspublishing.com

Additional copies of this workbook may be purchased online at:
www.outskirtspress.com/reflectionsdevotionalworkbook (Individual Sales)
www.outskirtspress.com/buybooks (Wholesale/Retail Sales)

ISBN: 978-0-9816765-3-1

Library of Congress Control Number: 2012905888

PRINTED IN THE UNITED STATES OF AMERICA

Devotion

This 'Devotional' Workbook has been 'divinely' created for :

_____
(Enter Your Name Here)

who has taken time out from their precious 'gift of life'
to
spend 'Time with God' alone

Table of Contents

From the Author

This 'devotional' workbook has been created for God's children (especially the brokenhearted and those that are bound) to draw nearer to Him. Yet, this is not a 'self-help' book. Man (we) will never be "fully" satisfied with 'self'; therefore, man cannot help 'self'. Jesus came to set the captives (us) free and once he frees us, we are free indeed; but only if we 'willfully' [help ourselves to] abide as part of the vine. (John 15:4-6).

We are all created by God (the 'heavenly' Father) and each child [believer] has a different relationship with Him. As you read the book "Reflections of A Spiritual Awakening" and I share my reflections of "life lessons" with you, use YOUR workbook (making journal entries) and begin reflecting (writing testimonials) on YOUR own "life lessons."

While reflecting, you will receive revelations [learning truth; gaining wisdom, knowledge and understanding - renewing your mind] of how God reaches out and touches each of us, every day, in His own special way. As the Holy Spirit leads you… evidence of 'works of the Lord' in YOUR life will evolve; drawing YOU into a (more) closer [covenant] relationship with God.

I bless and worship my 'heavenly' Father (God) daily, as well as meditate on His word and love for me. And after working on this assignment of great "honor" and "privilege" for you, I am fully persuaded He loves you too. God is love... and it is His desire that you learn to love Him just as much as He loves you! (Matthew 22:37 & 38.)

Peace and Blessings unto you! (And if not already), it is my prayer that you begin to declare "Psalm 66:16" in the remainder of YOUR 'spiritual' journey; always giving God the Glory!

Sheila Church-McSween

Your 'Devotional' Workbook:

Is a "teaching tool" and "spiritual journal" created to further YOUR understanding of the 'nature and context' of the book Reflections of A Spiritual Awakening.

Its **'Purpose'** is to "sow seeds of empowerment" to enrich YOUR life. And its **'Destiny'** is to bring YOU "spiritual prosperity" ["spiritual wealth"] once YOU embrace its content.

IT WILL:

➤ Enhance YOUR 'Reflections' of 'works of the Lord' in YOUR life (demonstrating the love of Jesus Christ) as YOU complete YOUR "testimonials of Life Lessons."

➤ Guide YOU towards 'true' Purpose & Destiny; God's 'will' ['Master Plan'] for YOUR life. [II Timothy 1:9]

    ▪ If you have <u>already</u> seen God's face, you will begin to see more of Him - instilling a deeper relationship with your 'heavenly' Father (God).

    ▪ If you have <u>never</u> seen God's face, He will begin to reveal Himself unto you - as you draw nearer unto Him. [John 14:21]

HOW TO USE IT:

➤ DO NOT treat YOUR Workbook as if it is a 'Diary' - inklings of ideas or thoughts penned on paper. However, DO keep YOUR Workbook in a private, safe place as if it is a 'Diary'.

➤ Always find a quiet, comfortable place <u>before</u> reading and reflecting (journaling) in YOUR Workbook.

➤ Always read the Book chapter <u>before</u> reflecting (journaling) in YOUR Workbook chapter.

➤ DO NOT read [skip] back and forth between Book chapters. [You must take time out to embrace both Book and YOUR Workbook in order to come into "a spiritual awakening" (revelation of truth, knowledge and understanding) from YOUR own "life lessons" God will reveal unto you].

➤ Keep YOUR Bible handy to review 'Scriptures' (in Book and Workbook). Evaluate 'Scriptures' comparing them to YOUR "life lessons." This will aide in your 'spiritual' growth and the development (perception) of 'spiritual' "vision and hearing" ["eyes to see" and "ears to hear"] of the Lord's (God's) presence in YOUR life.

Workbook Chapters include: SEGMENTS, SECTIONS and REFLECTIONS

➢ SEGMENTS: of "*My Reflections*" are generalized 'Reflections' pertaining to Chapter subject matters. Write in a response or mark the answer closely related to YOUR own 'Reflection' of Chapter subject matter.

Then, at the end of each **Segment**, check the (1) box you feel best identifies with YOUR overall 'Reflection' of Chapter subject matter.

➢ SECTIONS: contain personalized details of YOUR overall 'Reflections' to Chapter subject matters [the (1) box YOU selected at the end of the **Segment** - "*My Reflections*"]. Again, write in a response or mark the answer closely related to YOUR own 'Reflections' of subject matter. [Completing sections will lead to YOUR "testimonials of Life Lessons."]

❖ **Main Section Headers** within Workbook chapters are identified by these **'large'** bold diamonds, enclosed in black backgrounds. Complete only (1) Main Section per Chapter; the one that applies to you. Almost all Main Sections contain **Subsections.**

❖ **Subsections** within Main Sections are identified, and separated, by these **'smaller'** bold diamonds. Certain Subsections will not apply to you - DO NOT complete these sections.

➢ REFLECTIONS: are overviews of Chapter subject matters [life lessons].

Entering YOUR Reflections:

➢ There is no "right way" or "wrong way" to respond to 'Reflections'. They are YOUR 'afterthoughts' of predicaments and/or circumstances. And plus, no two (2) people respond alike; each person's perception will somewhat differ - although they may have faced the same challenge. YOUR only response to 'Reflections' should be an 'honest' response (identifying with your true, inner-self). Being 'honest' is the only way you will be 'set free' from the bondages in your thinking, your actions, your attitudes, and past traditions. And, is the only way you will draw nearer unto God.

➢ As you open up and draw nearer unto God, inspiration from the 'Holy Spirit' will guide you while completing YOUR Workbook... and YOUR Workbook will eventually "come to life" (given that you 'Reflect' honestly) transforming into a 'spiritual' journal "demonstrating the love of Jesus Christ" ["works of the Lord"] in YOUR life.

➢ Before entering YOUR first 'Reflection', take a long look at the image of 'the man in the mirror' [YOUR 'true' Reflection].

➢ After completing YOUR Workbook, take a second long look at 'the man in the mirror'. If you have embraced truth, you should see (visualize) yourself from a different perspective: 'The man in the mirror' should reflect an image of a person "fearfully and wonderfully made" (*Psalm139:14*).

Chapter 1

Dreams Deferred

"W hat do you want to be when you grow up?" I know this question sounds familiar ... It's that famous, legendary question we were all asked as children.

My Reflections:

As a child, I wanted to be _____ when I grew up!

My idea of the "American dream" was based on: (List the things that you desired out of life)

1 _____

2 _____

3 _____

4 _____

5 _____

6 _____

7 _____

My idea of the "American dream" was reachable. (What I desired to accomplish in life was realistic and attainable) _____ Yes _____ No

☐ I reached MY "American dream"; I am <u>presently</u> Living MY Dream.

☐ I reached MY "American dream"; except I am <u>no longer</u> Living My Dream.

☐ I <u>did not</u> reach MY "American dream"; My Dreams <u>have been</u> "Dreams Deferred."

➤ Complete (1) of (3) Main Sections based on YOUR response to the "American dream."

❖ **I am Presently Living MY Dream:** ☐

Testimonials

I am (did become) who/what I wanted to be as a child growing up. _____ Yes_____ No

I am satisfied [fulfilled] with my life. (Who/what I am now, including career wise, and choice(s) I have made) _____ Yes_____ No

In pursuit of achieving my dream, I did make some 'wrong' life choices. _____ Yes _____ No

If given a chance to relive my dream, I would do certain things differently. _____ Yes_____ No

Do you have 'new' dreams? _____ Yes_____ No

Are you continually in search of something? _____ Yes_____ No

Describe how you feel right now - as it relates to your life: (Be 'honest' with your inner-self).

_____

_____

_____

_____

_____

_____

❖ **I am No Longer Living MY Dream:** ☐

Testimonials

I am (did become) who/what I wanted to be as a child growing up. _____ Yes_____ No

I was satisfied [fulfilled] when I was living my dream. (Who/what I was, including career wise, and choice(s) I made) _____ Yes_____ No

I am satisfied [comfortable; content] with my life's present predicament. (Who I am now and my lifestyle) _____ Yes_____ No

After achieving my dream, I made several 'wrong' life choices. _____ Yes _____ No

If given a chance to relive my dream, I would you do certain things differently to keep my dream. _____ Yes_____ No

Are you willing to dream 'new' dreams? (Start life anew) _____ Yes _____ No

Are you continually in search of something? _____ Yes_____ No

Describe how you feel inside right now concerning your life: (Be *honest* with your inner-self).

_____

_____

_____

_____

_____

_____

❖ **MY Dreams have been "Dreams Deferred":** ☐

"Man's goings are of the Lord; how can a man then understand his own way?" - Proverb 20:24

Did you become who/what I wanted to be as a child growing up? _____ Yes_____ No

Are you content [at ease] with your life's present predicament? (Who you are now and your present lifestyle) _____ Yes_____ No

Did you accomplish any of your (adult) life's dreams [goals; desires]? _____ Yes _____ No

If certain (adult) life dreams <u>have</u> been accomplished, are you satisfied [pleased] with what you have accomplished thus far? _____ Yes _____ No

In pursuit of achieving your dream, did you make <u>many</u> wrong life choices? _____ Yes _____ No

Did you come close to achieving your dream (but pieces you thought were parts of the puzzle to your "American dream" just would not fit)? _____ Yes _____ No

What stopped you from achieving your dream? (Briefly list some of life's inner-most, unsettling predicaments or circumstances that occurred doing your 'pursuit of happiness' that you <u>think</u> may have hindered your dream):

1_____

2_____

3 _____

4 _____

5 _____

Do you share similar experiences of *"Dreams Deferred"* with the author?...

❖ **On some road along the way, did you lose your dream (hope)?** _____ Yes _____ No

| Respond to (1) of the (2) sections that apply to you: |

☐ **I Still Have Hope - MY dreams have been "deferred":**

| **Testimonials** |

"Dreams deferred" are similar to other people's "dreams that have been fulfilled."
_____ Yes _____ No

Ever wondered... "How life's dreams so simple, could be so hard to achieve?"
_____ Yes _____ No

Are you working towards fulfilling these "dreams that have been deferred"? _____ Yes _____ No

a) *Yes, I am working towards "dreams deferred":* ☐

Briefly explain how you kept hold of YOUR dream. (Why you have not [never] lost hope):

_____

_____

_____

_____

_____

_____

Did you believe that you were 'capable' of achieving your dream? (Having the ability and 'driving force' to accomplish it) _____ Yes _____ No

Did you believe that you were 'worthy' of such achievement(s)? (Deserving of the things that you desired and admired) _____ Yes _____ No

Compare your 'new' [right] paths today to paths of yesterday. (List at least (4) wrong turns of past; and (4) new roads you are traveling today):

Old Ways of Doing Things:	New Ways of Doing Things:
1.	1.
2.	2.
3.	3.
4.	4.

b) *No, I am __not__ working towards "dreams deferred":* ☐

How do you expect to keep YOUR dream [keep 'hope alive']? (Explain your plans for achieving your dream if you <u>are not</u> taking any steps towards walking into your destiny):

_____

_____

_____

_____

_____

_____

☐   **I <u>No Longer</u> Have Hope - I have lost MY dream:**

Can you remember which road you were traveling when you lost your dream? (The predicament or circumstance that occurred causing you to lose all hope) _____ Yes _____ No

Do you believe that God can 'resurrect' your dream? (Redirect your paths, turning "dreams deferred" into "dreams fulfilled") _____ Yes _____ No

If you <u>believe</u> that God can 'resurrect' your dream, would you be willing to dream (have hope) again? _____ Yes _____ No

a) *Yes, I would be willing to dream again:* ☐

If willing to dream again, briefly describe your dream. (Would they be "dreams deferred"; are you in search of 'new found' hope, etc.):

_____

_____

Do you believe [have faith] that you are 'capable' of achieving your dream? (That you can do all things through Christ who strengthens you!) _____ Yes _____ No

Do you believe [have faith] that you are 'worthy' of such achievements? (Deserving of things that you desire - things that are in God's will for you) _____ Yes _____ No

What would you do differently today, compared to yesterday, in order to achieve your dream? (List at least (4) wrong turns of your past; and (4) new roads you would take today):

Old Ways of Doing Things:	New Ways of Doing Things:
1.	1.
2.	2.
3.	3.
4.	4.

b) *No, I am not willing to dream again:* ☐

Have you [buried] your dream? _____ Yes _____ No

Are there things in life you (still) desire and/or admire? (Being closer to God; an abundant life; a new career; marriage; children, etc.) _____ Yes _____ No

If there are things in life you (still) desire and/or admire, briefly describe some of these things:

_____

_____

_____

If it was revealed to you that God has plans to 'resurrect' your dream (give you the things that you desire and/or admire), would this 'encourage' your hope (desire) of dreaming again? _____ Yes _____ No

If 'encouraged' to dream again: Would you be willing to seek (more of) God's face in order to achieve 'new' dreams (reach 'new heights')? _____ Yes _____ No

Reflections of Dreams Deferred:

If you have lost your dream [hope], continue to embrace this workbook ('reflecting' on YOUR own "Life Lessons"). And hopefully, like the author, you'll come into "A Spiritual Awakening" and dream again too!

Chapter Reflections: (Write additional thoughts/feelings about this Chapter here:)

_____

_____

_____

_____

_____

_____

Chapter 2

Valley of Dry Bones

*H*ave you ever been resurrected?

"And he said unto, Son of man, can these bones live? And I answered, O Lord God, thou knowest. Again he said unto me, Prophesy upon these bones, and say unto them, O ye dry bones, hear the word of the Lord. Thus saith the Lord God unto these bones; Behold, I will cause breath to enter into you, and you shall live." - Ezekiel 37:3 & 4.

My Reflections:

I know what it feels like to experience normal 'peaks' of "Valley Lo's" (life's 'ups and downs').
_____ Yes _____ No

I know what it feels like to fall victim to the prey of the enemy through various 'negative' strongholds ["spirits of vexations"]. _____ Yes _____ No

I know what it feels like to have someone 'out of the will of God' ['negative'] in your life (a hindrance; persecuting and crucifying.) _____ Yes _____ No

I know what it feels like to have a 'negative' spiritual force controlling (reigning) in your life.
_____ Yes _____ No

I know what it feels like to be 'spiritually' dead inside (loss of self-worth; brokenhearted; a void within - separated from God). _____ Yes _____ No

I know what it feels like to be 'resurrected' ('spiritually' born again). _____ Yes _____ No

- ☐ I am '<u>presently</u>' experiencing some of the above predicaments.
- ☐ I have '<u>past</u>' experiences relating to some of the above predicaments.
- ☐ I have 'never' experienced life in the "Valley of Dry Bones."

> If 'presently' experiencing any of these 'negative' predicaments:
>
> YOU are living in the *'Valley of Dry Bones'*!
>
> *"...behold they say, Our bones are dried, and our hope is lost: we are cut off for our parts."*
> (Ezekiel 37:11)

Many people do not evaluate their life predicaments or circumstances; they just live life. And people who do recognize their 'negative' predicaments or circumstances, and continue to live in them, may not understand they are living a form of bondage; being held captive - in 'Egypt'. We have been 'set free' from bondage (slavery and sin) through the 'precious' bloodshed by our Lord and Savior, Jesus Christ; God wants all of His children to live an abundant (upright, prosperous, healthy, joyful and peaceful) life.

Most people have a hard time admitting who they really are and how they really live life; living a life of 'self-denial' and like "love don't love nobody." People find certain life's predicaments or circumstances hard to think about, so they ignore them; hard to talk about, so they don't share them; let alone write about them. Writing is a form of freedom. Writing releases emotions (feelings). Writing about 'negative' emotions (feelings) releases hurt and pain harbored within. Plus, ignoring these types of predicaments and/or circumstances one will never reach their 'true' purpose and destiny in life.

In order to come into a 'spiritual awakening,' one must be 'honest' with their "inner-self" while responding to Reflections. Remember, this workbook was 'divinely' created for YOU; it does not have to be seen by anyone, nor do you have to 'Reflect' with anyone. While using YOUR workbook, YOU are spending 'Time with God' alone.

NOTE:

For 'Safety' Purposes: If presently living in a "life-threatening" predicament or circumstance [environment], DO NOT 'Reflect' (write) in this workbook.

However, you should at least 'Reflect' (by taking mental notes only) to determine who you really are, where you presently are in life and where your destiny is headed. [Share these things with God; He already knows who you really are (your true character), where you are (how you feel inside), and where you are headed (the road you are on). Only God can place you on the right path and reveal the 'true' purpose and destiny He has planned for you].

> Complete (1) of (3) Main Sections based on YOUR response to "Predicaments."

❖ **I am 'presently' living in the 'Valley of Dry Bones':** ☐

"Yea, though I walk through the valley of the shadow of death, I will fear no evil: for thou art with me; thy rod and thy staff they comfort me." - Psalm 23:4.

Testimonials

Identify the **form(s) of bondage:** ☐ *Psychological* (Emotional / Mental)   ☐ *Physical*

[Note: Physical bondage listed here does not give reference to physical disability]

Identify the **Source(s)** [and **Root Cause(s)**] of your bondage:

> Review all (3) **Sources** and **Root Causes**. In some cases, all (3) **Sources** may apply. And, more than (1) **Root Cause** - depending on how YOU live life.

❖ **I am 'presently' holding 'Myself' captive due to [CAUSE]:** ☐

❖ 'Dreams deferred' - my life did not turn out, or been, what I expected it to be. _____Yes_____ No

❖ Traumas' - of abuse, neglect, rejection, abandonment. _____ Yes _____ No

❖ 'Self-condemnation' - shame, hurt, or guilt concerning my past behavior. _____ Yes _____ No

❖ 'Self-hatred' - inability to accept or love myself. _____ Yes _____ No

I have lived in bondage (slavery; sin): _____ (Years; months).

Are you committing (any) sins against yourself? _____ Yes _____ No

Are you suffering from stressors of anxiety, panic attacks or depression? (Sick Within) _____ Yes _____ No

Are you suffering emotionally from "dreams deferred?" (Heartbroken; Sick Within) _____ Yes _____ No

Are you (or have you ever been) a "body snatcher"? (A mean-spirited or angry person, holding other people captive due to YOUR past or present predicaments or behavior) _____ Yes _____ No

Are you able to sleep (rest) peacefully at night? _____ Yes _____ No

Have you shared these feelings or predicament with anyone or sought some form of help? _____ Yes _____ No

Are you taking any type of prescription medications? _____ Yes _____ No

Would you consider your predicament and/or circumstance to be 'life-threatening'? _____ Yes _____ No

How long have you had these feelings or been in this predicament? (_____)

[**Note:** If it's been too long or 'life-threatening' - you may need some form of therapy: Toll Free HOT LINE NUMBER: National Mental Health: 1-800-969-6642]

Do you have a (personal) relationship with God? _____ Yes _____ No

Although it 'rains on the just and the unjust' *(Matthew 5:45)* <u>and</u> 'all things come alike to all' *(Ecclesiastes 9:2)*: Do you think your experience in the 'Valley of Dry Bones' may be due to some of the 'negative' choices you made in life? _____ Yes _____ No

Are you 'willing and ready' to be resurrected (delivered; set free) from your predicament and/or circumstance? _____ Yes _____ No

[**Note:** All you need is 'faith' the size of a grain of mustard seed - to move any mountain that stands in your way. Meditate on the Law, mainly Scriptures of *Psalms 119:1-176*].

❖ **I am *'presently'* being held captive by 'Someone else' due to [CAUSE]:** ☐

> For 'safety' purposes, certain [response] sections have been eliminated. For 'deliverance' purposes, it is imperative that you identify (acknowledge) your present predicament and/or circumstance. **Take mental notes only**.

- ❖ Acting as their 'enabler' (co-dependent) - supporting their afflictions and addictions.

- ❖ Mental/Emotional (verbal) abuse - being yelled at, screamed at, called names, blamed for everything, humiliated and shamed; Isolated, intimidated, and controlled.

- ❖ Physical abuse - afflicted with physical pain, causing injuries to my body.

- ❖ Sexual abuse - forced to participate in unwanted, unsafe, or degrading sexual activity.

- ❖ Doing things for this person that I have never done for anyone else, including myself.

- ❖ Accepting things from this person that I have never accepted from anyone else - their continuous immoral behavior, causing me degradation and humiliation.

Would you consider this person to be a "body snatcher"?

I have lived in fear/bondage (slavery; sin): _____ (Years; months).

Would you consider your predicament and/or circumstance to be 'life-threatening'? (Are you afraid of this person?)

Have you 'spiritually' died over, and over, and over again - continually being persecuted and crucified - hoping to save this person, while waiting on somebody else (really 'Jesus') to come and save you?

Are you able to sleep (rest) peacefully at night?

Do you have a (personal) relationship with God? _____ Yes _____ No

Although it 'rains on the just and the unjust' *(Matthew 5:45)* and 'all things come alike to all' *(Ecclesiastes 9:2):* Do you think your experience in the 'Valley of Dry Bones' may be due to some of the 'negative' choices you made in life? _____ Yes _____ No

Are you 'willing and ready' to be resurrected (delivered, set free) from your predicament and/or circumstance? Can you or have you sought help?

Toll Free HOT LINE NUMBER: National Domestic Violence Hotline:

1-800-799-SAFE (7233)

Being "persecuted and crucified" in 'unjustified, death-defying' predicaments:

SOMEONE IS IN YOUR LIFE THAT IS 'OUT OF THE WILL OF GOD'!

Let God "resurrect" you! (Bring "redemption and righteous justification")
No one should ever live in fear or in bondage; Jesus has set us free! "If the Son therefore make you free, ye shall be free indeed" - *John 8:36.* Meditate on (study) the Scriptures of *Ezekiel 37:1-14; Psalms 23, 27, 91 & 119; Matthew 5; John 11; and Romans 5 & 6.*

❖ **I am *'presently'* being held captive by `Something else` due to [CAUSE]:** ☐

For 'privacy' purposes, certain [response] sections have been eliminated. For 'deliverance' purposes, it is imperative you identify (acknowledge) your present predicament(s) and/or circumstance(s) and respond to certain sections - If you prefer, **take mental notes only.**

- ❖ A Mental Disorder - of depression, bipolar, schizophrenia, etc.

- ❖ An Addiction - to drugs, alcohol, nicotine, sex, food, gambling, etc.

- ❖ 'Immoral' behavior - biblically inappropriate and/or what society shuns.

❖ Tormenting nightmares - causing me to awake from my sleep in 'fear.'

❖ A Phobia [fear] - paralyzing me and limiting certain or daily activities.

❖ Something other than the above: (Enter response here) _____.

I have lived in fear/bondage (slavery; sin): _____ (Years; months).

Could these be 'negative' forces [vexing spirits; negative strongholds] warring against YOUR spirit, trying to control YOUR thought patterns? _____ Yes _____ No

Are you able to sleep (rest) peacefully at night? _____ Yes _____ No

Would you consider your predicament and/or circumstance to be 'life-threatening'? _____ Yes _____ No

Do you have a (personal) relationship with God? _____ Yes _____ No

Although it 'rains on the just and the unjust' *(Matthew 5:45)* <u>and</u> 'all things come alike to all' *(Ecclesiastes 9:2)*: Do you think your experience in the 'Valley of Dry Bones' may be due to some of the negative choices you made in life? _____ Yes _____ No

Are you 'willing and ready' to be resurrected (delivered, set free) from your predicament and/or circumstance? _____ Yes _____ No

Have you sought help? _____ Yes _____ No

Are you taking any type of prescription medications? _____ Yes _____ No

Toll Free HOT LINE NUMBERS:
National Drug Abuse Hotline: 1-800-662-HELP (4357)
Alcoholics Anonymous - US: 1-877-515-1255
National Mental Health: 1-800-969-6642

<u>Note:</u> No one should ever live in fear or in bondage; Jesus has set us free! "If the Son therefore shall make you free, ye shall be free indeed" - *John 8:36*. Meditate on *Ezekiel 37:1-14* and *Psalms 23, 27, 91 & 119*.

❖ **I have 'lived' in the 'Valley of Dry Bones' :** ☐

Testimonials

Although I have come out from that place, experience in the 'Valley of Dry Bones' was due to [CAUSE]:

- ☐ Holding *myself* captive
- ☐ *Someone else* holding me captive
- ☐ *Something else* holding me captive
- ☐ A combination of the above

[**Note**: If you need help identifying [CAUSE], review **Source(s)** [and **Root Cause(s)**] in the (3) Subsections of "*Presently* living in the *Valley of Dry Bones*" (pgs. 10-13).]

Do you know what it feels like to be 'resurrected' (brought back to life after being 'spiritually' dead for so long)? _____ Yes _____ No

Did you suffer emotionally; were you heartbroken (sick within) from "dreams deferred"? _____ Yes _____ No

Did you suffer mentally; (sick within) from stressors of anxiety, panic attacks and/or depression? _____ Yes _____ No

Did you suffer physically; from a form of abuse or your body responded negatively to its 'negative' environment? _____ Yes _____ No

If you suffered emotionally, mentally or physically, briefly describe how you managed this sickness within or release from physical abuse. (Medication, therapy, intervention, etc.):

_____

_____

_____

_____

Briefly describe a 'trying' predicament or circumstance concerning family life, a personal relationship, an incident at work, financial difficulty, etc. you were involved in that you did not see a way out, but made it through it:

_____

_____

_____

_____

_____

_____

Briefly describe a "life-threatening" predicament or circumstance (psychological or physical) that occurred in your life that you did not see a way out, but made it through it:

_____

_____

_____

_____

_____

_____

_____

Was there a 'negative' force reigning in your life? (A vexing spirit; stronghold of some sort controlling your thought patterns) _____ Yes _____ No_____ Not Sure

Was there ever a special time when someone provided you comfort? (A person who had been where you were (in your predicament) and you knew that this person truly understood how you felt inside) _____ Yes _____ No

If there __was__ a special person:

Did you already know this person? _____ Yes _____ No

Briefly describe how this person provided you comfort - helped you make it through; turning a 'trying time' into a 'special time':

_____

_____

_____

_____

_____

_____

❖ **Was there a person 'out of the will of God' in your life?** _____ Yes _____ No

> ➤ DO NOT complete this section if YOUR response was **'No'**

Was this person 'reigning' in your life (even controlling your thought patterns)? _____ Yes _____ No

Did you do things for this person that you had never done for anyone else, including yourself? _____ Yes _____ No

Did you accept things from this person that you had never accepted from anyone else? (Their continuous immoral behavior, causing you degradation and humiliation, and loss of self-worth) _____ Yes _____ No

Did you 'spiritually' die (being persecuted and crucified) over, and over, and over again for this one person's sins before redeeming yourself? _____ Yes _____ No

Were you righteously redeemed? (Becoming part of the vine - no longer living life apart from the Father) _____ Yes _____ No

[If comfortable enough, write about this predicament. Briefly describe when, where, and what happened:

_____

_____

_____

_____

_____

_____]

When did you become aware of the enemy's tactics (stronghold or presence) in your life?
_____ While in this predicament or, _____ After coming out of this predicament.

Were you a child when certain of these predicaments occurred? _____ Yes _____ No

Did you forgive this person (or these people) for their trespasses/transgressions against you?
_____ Yes _____ No

❖ **After coming out of the 'Valley' ...being set free:**

Did your desire to live become great? _____ Yes _____ No

Did you ever return? (Look back; get involved in the same (or another) predicament again)
_____ Yes _____ No

Are you now able to discern the enemy's subtle presence (especially working through a person)?
_____ Yes _____ No

Did you find YOUR reflections ["life lessons"] of life in the 'Valley of Dry Bones' hard to think about, let alone write about? _____ Yes _____ No

Would you be willing to share YOUR experiences in the 'Valley of Dry Bones' with someone else?
(Minister to help other people) _____ Yes _____ No

❖ **Do you believe it was God who 'divinely' intervened in your life?**
_____ Yes _____ No _____ Not Sure

> ➤ Respond to (1) of (3) based on YOUR response to 'Intervention':

☐ **I believe God 'divinely' intervened:**

I prayed to God on a regular basis while in this predicament. _____ Yes _____ No

My prayers supplications were heard in heaven. _____ Yes _____ No

I experienced the 'supernatural' powers of the Holy Spirit while in this predicament.
_____ Yes _____ No

"I have been resurrected!" (Brought back to life after being 'spiritually' dead inside)
_____ Yes _____ No

If you <u>have</u> been resurrected:

Were you 'righteously' redeemed? (Died to your own sins [flesh] and the 'Holy Spirit' now dwell within) _____ Yes _____ No

What did God do to help you overcome your predicament? (Briefly describe your deliverance from living in the 'Valley of Dry Bones'):

_____

_____

_____

_____

☐ **I *do not* believe God 'divinely' intervened:**

I considered it 'luck' to have overcome my predicament(s). _____ Yes _____ No

I believe that all things eventually work themselves out. _____ Yes _____ No

What did YOU do <u>or</u> what measures were taken to overcome your predicament? (Briefly describe your deliverance from living in the 'Valley of Dry Bones'):

_____

_____

_____

_____

☐ **I am _not sure_ if God 'divinely' intervened:**

I prayed to God on a regular basis while in this predicament. _____ Yes _____ No

Do you believe your prayer supplications were heard in Heaven? _____ Yes _____ No

Is there "doubt" (a lack of knowledge and faith) on your part concerning the 'supernatural' powers of the Holy Spirit? _____ Yes _____ No

What did YOU do or what measures were taken to overcome your predicament? (Briefly describe your deliverance from living in the 'Valley of Dry Bones'):

_____

_____

_____

_____

❖ **I have 'never' lived in the 'Valley of Dry Bones':** ☐

Testimonials

❖ *Although I have had 'valley experiences' (low 'peaks' in life):*

I have never experienced any 'strongholds' of emotional or mental bondage. _____Yes _____No

I have never experienced any 'strongholds' of abuse [mental, physical or sexual].
_____ Yes _____ No

I sleep (rest) peacefully at night. (Have 'sweet' sleep) _____ Yes _____ No

I have a relationship with God. _____ Yes _____ No

I consider myself to be blessed. _____ Yes _____ No

❖ *Although it 'rains on the just and on the unjust' [Matthew 5:45] and 'all things come alike to all' [Ecclesiastes 9:2]:*

Do you think not having experienced living life in the 'Valley of Dry Bones' thus far is due to 'positive' choices you have made in life? _____ Yes _____ No

Have you "thanked" ["blessed"] God (counted your blessings) to this day for His mercy and grace (protection and favor) to have never lived in the 'Valley of Dry Bones'?
_____ Yes _____ No

Reflections of Valley of Dry Bones:

> If you completed "testimonials": You now have YOUR own 'Reflections' of "Jehovah-Nissi" - the "Lord that reigns in Victory!" *(Exodus 17:15&16).*
>
> If you have come out from that place (the 'Valley of Dry Bones') it was "Jehovah-Nissi" - the "Lord that reigns in Victory" who 'divinely' intervened! DO NOT let the enemy continue to deceive YOU and/or steal from YOU!

✓ There are many 'unbelievers' concerning Resurrection of life. And of the scores of people who do believe in Resurrection of life, many have difference of opinions when it comes to defining the word [term] and forms [types] of Resurrections. Even so, listed here are two (2) forms of Resurrection the author concludes as 'safe' to include in this workbook:

1) The Resurrection that takes place in the 'physical body' of man after being spiritually born again [Spiritual resurrection] - a change made within the spirit (inner; soul of) man. (Ezekiel 11:19-20, 36:24-36, 37:1-14; John 3:5-6; and Colossians 2:11-14 & 3:1-5.)

2) The Resurrection that takes place in the 'physical form' of man after the fleshly body actually dies [Bodily resurrection] - resurrected [raised] in a different [spiritual] body. (Mark 16:6-7; Luke 24; John 11:25-26; I Corinthians 15:20-23 & 15:42-52; and Revelation 20:4-6.)

✓ Man (we) will never be "fully" satisfied with 'self'. Man (we) will remain in bondage to 'self' [sin; "voids" within] until being born again.

✓ Man (we) must deny 'self' [die to the flesh] in order to allow the 'Holy Spirit' to do a work in [resurrect] him (us); by putting on the 'new' man - being reborn into God's (His own) image (Genesis 1:27; Luke 9:23; John 15:4-6; and Romans 12:3).

Chapter Reflections: (Write additional thoughts/feelings about this Chapter here:)

_____

_____

_____

_____

_____

_____

Chapter 3

Time with God

In the "End Time" will your time with God really matter... at the time that matters most to Him?

As a result of having this workbook in your hand right now, I will presume you already know Jesus; God's Beloved Son, our Lord and Saviour (the 'Anointed One'). Jesus saves! [John 6:35, 8:12, 10:9, 11, 11:25-26]. And, the only way to the Father is through His Son [John 14:6 & 15:1; Hebrews 12:2; and I John 2:23].

If you have never used a journal for making 'spiritual' entries, at this very moment you are taking another step towards a more personal [intimate; covenant] relationship with God [Jehovah; Lord (Exodus 6:3; Psalm 83:18)]... drawing nearer unto Him. YOUR Reflections (journal entries) will eventually "come to life"... making God visible; strengthening your faith - allowing you to grow greater in grace.

My Reflections:

I know who I am. _____ Yes _____ No

I know God. _____ Yes _____ No

I know my reason for existence. _____ Yes _____ No

I spend 'Time with God' alone. _____ Yes _____ No

- ☐ I know Who I Am; know God; and My Reason for Existence.
- ☐ I know Who I Am; know God; but not My Reason for Existence.
- ☐ I know Who I Am; but do not know God or My Reason for Existence.
- ☐ I do not know Who I Am, God, or My Reason for Existence.

❖ **I know Who I Am; know God; and My Reason for Existence:** ☐

Testimonials

Who are YOU? (Describe who you feel you are from a 'spiritual' perspective. Do not include professional titles or an ascribed status):

_____

_____

_____

_____

_____

_____

What do YOU know about God? (Who is He? Describe Him as you know Him):

_____

_____

_____

_____

_____

_____

Are you a person of faith; a believer and follower of Jesus Christ? _____ Yes_____ No

Do you attend Church (to fellowship, praise, and worship God)? _____ Yes_____ No

If you <u>attend</u> Church, how often do you attend? ____ Days a week / or ____ Days a month.

Do you have a Church home? (Are you a member of a Church?) _____ Yes_____ No

If you <u>have</u> a Church home, do you serve in a position in the Church? _____ Yes_____ No

If you <u>serve</u> in the Church, in what position(s) do you serve?

➤ I serve in the position(s) of: _____

❖ **Briefly describe YOUR relationship with God:**

Who is He to YOU? <u>and</u> Who are YOU to Him?

_____

_____

_____

_____

How do you <u>think</u> God would describe you - seeing your 'present' character traits and/or attributes, and how you live life? (Be honest with your inner-self):

_____

_____

_____

In describing how you <u>think</u> God sees you now, do you think He is pleased with you as His child?
_____ Yes _____ No

[If you <u>do not</u> think that God is pleased with you as His child, briefly explain why?

_____

_____

_____]

Which 'biblical' description best describes how people 'presently' see you: (What have people [family, friends and acquaintances] told you about your character traits and/or attributes? How you relate to <u>and</u> treat people; how you live life. Be 'honest' with your inner-self).

a) As a child of God ☐　　　**b)** As a lost sheep ☐　　**c)** As a child living in darkness ☐

If your response to how <u>people</u> see you 'differs' from how you think <u>God</u> sees you, explain why people see you differently:

_____

_____

_____

If your response of how <u>people</u> see you 'differs' from how <u>you</u> see yourself:

1) Is the person that people 'presently' see who you really are? (Your true character)
_____ Yes_____ No

2) Are you living a life of 'self-deception'? (Pretending to be who you really want to be, in 'self-denial' of who you really are) _____ Yes_____ No

3) Are you a 'religious' person, practicing 'vain' religion? (Having a form of godliness, but denying the power thereof - *II Timothy 3:5*) _____ Yes_____ No

❖ **Why do YOU exist?**

Briefly explain your purpose for living: (What are you here to do while living in this earthly realm?)

_____

_____

_____

_____

❖ **If YOU know God:**

a) Does God know YOU? _____ Yes_____ No

b) Do YOU spend 'Time with God' alone? _____ Yes_____ No

❖ <mark>**I know Who I Am; know God; but _not_ My Reason for Existence:**</mark> ☐

Testimonials

Who are YOU? (Briefly describe who you feel you are from a 'spiritual' perspective. Do not include professional titles or an ascribed status)

_____

_____

_____

_____

_____

What do YOU know about God? (Who is He? Describe Him as YOU know Him):

_____

_____

_____

_____

Are you a person of faith; a believer <u>and</u> follower of Jesus Christ? _____ Yes_____ No

Do you attend Church (to fellowship, praise, and worship God)? _____ Yes_____ No

If you <u>attend</u> Church, how often do you attend? _____ Days a week / or _____ Days a month.

Do you have a Church home? (Are you a member of a Church)? _____ Yes_____ No

If you <u>have</u> a Church home, do you serve in a position in the Church? _____ Yes_____ No

If you <u>serve</u> in the Church, in what position(s) do you serve?

➤ I serve in the position(s) of: _____

❖ **Briefly describe YOUR relationship with God:**

Who is He to YOU? and Who are YOU to Him?

_____
_____
_____
_____

How do you <u>think</u> God would describe YOU - seeing your present character traits and/or attributes and how you live life? (Be 'honest' with your inner-self):

_____
_____
_____

In describing how you <u>think</u> God sees you now, do you think He is pleased with YOU as His child? _____ Yes _____ No

[**Note:** If you <u>do not</u> think that God is pleased with YOU, do you care to explain why?...

_____
_____
_____]

Which 'biblical' description best describes how people 'presently' see you: (What have people [family, friends and acquaintances] told you about your character traits and/or attributes? How you relate to and treat people; how you live life. Be 'honest' with your inner-self).

a) As a child of God ☐   **b)** As a lost sheep ☐   **c)** As a child living in darkness ☐

If your response to how <u>people</u> see you 'differs' from how you think <u>God</u> sees you, explain why people see you differently:

_____

_____

_____

_____

If your response of how <u>people</u> see you now 'differs' from how <u>you</u> see yourself:

1) Is the person that people 'presently' see who you really are? (Your true character)
_____ Yes_____ No

2) Are you living a life of 'self-deception'? (Pretending to be who you really want to be, in 'self-denial' of who you really are) _____ Yes_____ No

3) Are you a 'religious' person, practicing 'vain' religion? (Having a form of godliness, but denying the power thereof - *II Timothy 3:5*) _____ Yes_____ No

❖ **Why do YOU think YOU exist?**

Try to explain your purpose for living: (What do you <u>think</u> you are here to do while living in this earthly realm?)

_____

_____

_____

_____

❖ **If YOU know God, but <u>do not</u> know YOUR true 'reason for existence':**

Do YOU spend <u>any</u> 'Time with God' alone? _____ Yes_____ No

Do you consider yourself to have a personal [covenant] relationship with God?
_____ Yes_____ No

Could God have <u>already</u> revealed your 'purpose for life' and you did not have "eyes to see" or "ears to hear"? _____ Yes_____ No

Are you wrestling with God (Doing things your way, and not His)? _____ Yes_____ No

Do you think you need to look a little closer? (Draw nearer to Him) _____ Yes_____ No

❖ **I know Who I Am; but _do not_ know God _or_ My Reason for Existence:** ☐

> It is "impossible" to know Who YOU really Are, and NOT know GOD!
>
> - This is a GRAY area in YOUR life -
>
> (Things should be either 'black' or 'white')
> - Go to the NEXT Section -

❖ **I _do not_ know Who I Am, God _or_ My Reason for Existence:** ☐

Testimonials

Who do YOU think YOU are? (Describe who you feel you are from a 'spiritual' perspective. Do not include professional titles or an ascribed status):

_____

_____

_____

_____

_____

_____

Describe God to the best of your ability: (What you read, heard, or been taught about Him)

_____

_____

_____

_____

Would you consider yourself to be a person of faith? (A 'believer' in Jesus Christ)
_____ Yes_____ No

Are you a 'babe' in Christ? (Just getting to know Jesus; recently coming unto the Father as "a little child" - Hebrews 5:12 & 13). _____ Yes_____ No

Do you attend Church (to fellowship, praise, and worship God)? _____ Yes_____ No

If you <u>attend</u> Church, how often do you attend? ____ Days a week /or ____ Days a month.

Do you have a Church home (membership in a particular Church)? _____Yes_____ No

If you <u>have </u>a Church home, do you serve in a position in the Church? _____ Yes_____ No

If you <u>serve</u> in the Church, in what position(s) do you serve?

➢ I serve in the position(s) of: _____.

┌───┐
│ Respond to this next question **ONLY** if you │
│ Attend Church and/or Serve in the Church   │
└───┘

If you attend Church and/or serve in a position in the Church: Why do you think it is that you do not know God (have a personal [covenant] relationship with Him)? Explain YOUR predicament:

_____

_____

_____

_____

[**Note:** You could be suffering from "Failure to Thrive." After completing YOUR Workbook, you will begin to "see" more of Him and "draw nearer" unto Him.]

❖ **DO YOU know that God knows YOU? ...**

Whether you know it or believe it - God knows you: How do you <u>think</u> God would describe you - seeing your present character traits and/or attributes, and how you live life? (Be 'honest' with your inner-self):

_____

_____

_____

_____

In describing how you <u>think</u> God sees you at present, do you think He would be pleased with YOU as His child? _____Yes _____ No

[If you <u>do not</u> think that God would be pleased with YOU: Do you care to explain why?...

_____

_____

_____.]

Which 'biblical' description best describes how people 'presently' see you: (What have people [family, friends and acquaintances] told you about your character traits and/or attributes? How you relate to <u>and</u> treat people; how you live life. Be 'honest' with your inner-self).

a) As a child of God ☐   **b)** As a lost sheep ☐   **c)** As a child living in darkness ☐

If your response of how <u>people</u> see you 'differs' from how you think <u>God</u> would see you, explain why people see you differently:

_____

_____

_____

If your response of how <u>people</u> see 'differs' from how <u>you</u> see yourself:

1) Is the person that people see who you really are? (Your true character) _____ Yes_____ No

2) Are you living a life of 'self-deception'? (Pretending to be who you really want to be, in self-denial of who you really are) _____ Yes_____ No

3) Are you a 'religious' person, practicing 'vain' religion? (Having a form of godliness, but denying the power thereof - *II Timothy 3:5*) _____ Yes_____ No

❖ **Why do YOU think YOU exist?**

Try to explain your purpose for living: (What do you <u>think</u> you are here to do while living in this earthly realm?):

_____

_____

_____

❖ **Since YOU _do not_ know Who YOU _really_ are; God; or your 'Reason for Existence':**

a) Do you need to look a little closer? (Start spending 'Time with God'). _____ Yes_____ No

b) Do you understand what it takes to establish a [covenant] relationship with God? _____ Yes_____ No

c) Have YOU ever spent <u>any</u> 'Time with God' alone? _____ Yes_____ No

'Time with God'

"He that hath my commandments, and keepeth them, he it is that loveth me: and he that loveth me shall be loved of my Father, and I will love him, and will manifest myself to him." - John 14:21.

> ➤ Complete (1) of (2) Main Sections based on YOUR previous response to "Time With God":

❖ **I spend 'Time with God' alone:** ☐

Which is most important to you?

☐ Belief in Jesus Christ; ☐ Relationship with God; or ☐ Both

Explain why you chose your response:

_____

_____

_____

Did you notice how 'honest, personal and intimate' the author's journal entries were, while spending (private) 'time with God' alone? _____Yes _____ No

Did you notice the differences in the author's prayer [journal] entries (prayers of faith, praise & worship; prayers for protection; prayers of supplication/requests)? _____Yes _____ No

Did you notice the times (early morning hours) when most of the author's journal entries were written? _____Yes _____ No

Testimonials

I pray on a regular/daily basis. _____ Yes _____ No

I have confidence that when I pray, my prayers are heard in 'heaven.' _____ Yes _____ No

I have prayers that have been answered ["answered prayer requests"]. _____ Yes _____ No

I talk to God plainspoken and forthright at times. _____ Yes _____ No

I spend 'time with God: Daily ☐ Weekly ☐ Often ☐ Sometimes ☐

I have set 'times' I spend with God (mornings, evenings, etc.) _____ Yes_____ No

I have a set 'length of time' I spend with God (hours, minutes). _____ Yes_____ No

I spend 'Time with God' out of my love and devotion to Him. _____ Yes_____ No

List other form(s) of communication that you use to spend "Time with God" alone:

_____   _____

_____   _____

_____   _____

While spending 'Time with God' alone, have you ever felt His presence (the Spirit of the Lord)? _____ Yes_____ No

If you have felt His presence:

Were you surprised when you first felt the Spirit of the Lord? _____ Yes_____ No

Describe the atmosphere and how the Lord's presence made/or makes you feel:

_____

_____

❖ **I *do not* spend 'Time with God' alone:** ☐

Testimonials

Which is most important to you?
☐ Belief in Jesus Christ; ☐ Relationship with God; or ☐ Both

Explain why you chose your response:

_____

_____

_____

Did you notice how 'honest, personal and intimate' the author's journal entries were, while spending 'Time with God' alone? _____ Yes _____ No

Did you notice the differences in the author's prayer [journal] entries (prayers of faith, praise & worship; prayers for protection; prayers of supplication/requests)? _____ Yes _____ No

Did you notice the times (early morning hours) when most of the author's journal entries were written? _____ Yes _____ No

Besides getting to know Jesus (God's Son), are you aware that God wants YOU (His child) to establish a personal [covenant] relationship with Him as well? _____Yes _____ No

Have you ever asked yourself, or anyone else, "How does one get to know God?" (Establish a relationship with Him) _____Yes _____ No

Have you ever spent <u>any</u> 'Time with God' alone to pray? _____Yes _____ No

Have you ever had <u>any</u> 'personal' prayers that have been answered ("answered prayer requests")? _____ Yes _____ No

["*Ask, and it shall be given you; seek, and ye shall find; knock, and it shall be opened unto you*" - Matthew 7:7; Luke 11:9.]

Are you willing to spend more 'Time with God' alone, other than using this 'devotional' workbook (to 'reflect' on and increase 'works of the Lord' in your life)? _____Yes_____ No

If <u>willing</u> to spend more 'Time with God' alone:

What other form(s) of communication would you use to further aide in your establishing a [covenant] relationship with God?

_____   _____

_____   _____

_____   _____

- Many people go about doing "the Lord's [God's] work" on a daily basis, but never take time out to spend Time with God.

- The more time you spend with God, the more 'spiritually' you will [mature] and develop a deeper understanding of who God 'really' is; who YOU 'really' are; where YOU 'really' come from; and why YOU 'really' exist. But YOU must first get to know His Son...

  Because, in the "End Time" - YOU wouldn't want to be the one He professes, "*I never knew you: depart from me, ye that work iniquity*" (Matthew 7:23).

If you completed "testimonials": You now have YOUR own 'Reflections' of "Immanuel" - God with us! *(Isaiah 7:14 & Matthew 1:23)*

God's Character:

✓ God is "all-powerful"; "all-knowing"; and "everywhere". For those of you unaware, here are a few Scriptures to learn more about God: Psalm 103:6-19; Matthew 6:9-13; John 1:1-4; James 1:17-18.

✓ Without acknowledging Jesus Christ for who He really is (the Son of God; divinity), it is impossible to know (obtain favor from) God.

✓ God knows all of His children - regardless of whether you think He knows you or not.

✓ God loves all of His children - regardless of how you see yourself, how you think He sees you, or how you think people see you. God is Love and loves all that He has created. It is up to us whether we love Him back.

The Church [The Body of Christ]:

✓ The children of God (people) are the church [the body of Christ] (I Corinthians 12:27). Jesus Christ is head of the church [the chief corner stone] (I Corinthians 11:3; Ephesians 5:23; Colossians 1:18). *"For we are labourers together with God: ye are God's husbandry, ye are God's building"* - I Corinthians 3:9.

✓ The church [the body of Christ] was called by the will of God (I Corinthians 1:2, 1:9; Ephesians 2:8-10; I Thessalonians 2:4; II Thessalonians 1:4, 2:13-14); its members are new creations [creatures] in Christ (II Corinthians 5:17). The church was founded by Jesus Christ (Matthew 1:21; I Corinthians 3:11; Ephesians 3:19-21); the new blood covenant - "living letter" (Isaiah 11; Jeremiah 31:31-35; Ezekiel 34:23-31) replacing the old covenant of Moses - "letter of laws." The church's foundation was laid by apostles and prophets (Matthew 16:18; Ephesians 2:19-22), although its body has many members (Romans 8:4-5; I Corinthians 10:32; Ephesians 4:4-6; Galatians 3:28). *"But he that is joined unto the Lord is one spirit"* - I Corinthians 6:17.

✓ Although the 'body' is the "true temple of God" (I Corinthians 6:19-20), people assemble in churches (buildings and homes) for 'spiritual' fellowship and to give praise and worship unto the Lord [God] (Philippians 1:27; I Timothy 3:15; Hebrews 10:24-25). Spiritual gifts are for bringing unity to [the body of Christ] and more people into the church (Ephesians 4:11-13).

Time with God:

✓ The 'human' spirit (natural man) is not capable of worshiping God 'in Spirit and in Truth' (John 4:24). Natural man is 'unconscious' of the things of God until he is born again by the 'Holy Spirit' in the likeness of Him (Romans 5:19 & 8:5-8; I Corinthians 2:14; and I John 4).

✓ Although there are no set times when a person can come unto the 'heavenly' Father, it is a known fact that 'early morning hours' are times when:

- the Spirit of the Lord is highly elevated; God's presence is soaring. (As when the Lord gave Moses instructions for the commandments while in the desert of Sinai [Exodus 19 & 34]);

- the majority of God's children spend 'Time with God' alone. (As an early riser and starting each day with the Lord, prayer supplications have proven to be most effectual.) [Review the following scriptures : Genesis 32:24-29; Joshua 3:1, 6:12, 7:16, 8:10; Job 1:5; Psalms 88:13 & 119:147; and Mark 1:35].

✓ **Prayer Supplications**: Prayer's of the righteous availeth much. Prayer brings redemption, blessings, protection, etc. (Remember, David prayed always unto the Lord - Book of Psalms). Listed are a few Scriptures concerning these various types of prayers (Matthew 6:5-13; Psalm 23; Proverb 15:29; Luke 18:1; and Ephesians 6:18.)

✓ **Unanswered Prayer Requests**: The Lord [God] will not [grant] 'anything' or 'everything' that we pray for; ONLY things that are in His 'perfect' will (plan) for us. "You ask, and receive not, because you ask amiss..." (*James 4:3*). "God's thoughts are not our thoughts" and "His ways are higher than our ways" (*Isaiah 55:8-9*).

✓ **Power in Writing**: Writing brings freedom. Writing declarations and proclamations of what we desire out of life brings the same power as if these [words] were spoken words. God commanded many to write - that which was spoken and what was seen. "And the Lord answered and said, Write the vision and make it plain upon tables, that he may run that readeth it" (*Habakkuk 2:2*).

- Before reflecting further into this workbook, if you do not have a [separate] private journal for making 'spiritual' entries, you may want to purchase one. And as the 'Spirit of the Lord' leads you while 'reflecting' on past "life lessons," make entries of new prayer requests [supplications], dreams dreamed, visions seen, circumstances and/or predicaments that occur.

- Keep track of these entries (review them) and overtime, you can see and will feel 'works of the Lord' (God's presence) in your life.

[**Note:** Taking these small steps will be progress towards "Renewing Your Mind."]

Chapter Reflections: (Write additional thoughts/feelings about this Chapter here:)

_____

_____

_____

_____

_____

_____

Chapter 4

Purpose & Destiny Revealed

What is it that we really seek that our joy might be full? Most often, people go throughout life making decisions based on their "emotions" [heart] and "five senses" [gates to the soul] and then change their mind in a moment's notice when they "feel or sense" something else; not knowing what they really seek - instead of learning to wait on God (the gatekeeper) for His divine guidance; which can be revealed through the "gift of prophecy."

"Believe in the Lord your God, so shall ye be established (kept safe); believe his prophets, so shall ye prosper (succeed)" - II Chronicles 20:20.

My Reflections:

I believe in Jesus, God's 'beloved' Son; and have accepted God as my 'heavenly' Father.
_____ Yes _____ No

My 'true' life's "Purpose" has been revealed unto me. (God's intentional plans; reason for being)
_____ Yes _____ No

My 'true' life's "Destiny" has been revealed unto me. (God's work; expectations of me)
_____ Yes _____ No

I need to look a little closer (search my heart, to seek God's heart - in order for Him to receive me).
_____ Yes _____ No

I believe 'true' Purpose & Destiny can be revealed through the 'gift of Prophecy'.
_____ Yes _____ No

☐ God is my 'heavenly' Father; I know my 'true' Purpose & Destiny.
☐ God is my 'heavenly' Father; but I <u>do not</u> know my 'true' Purpose & Destiny.

> ➤ Complete (1) of (2) Main Sections based on YOUR response to "Purpose & Destiny."

❖ **God is my 'heavenly' Father; I know my 'true' Purpose & Destiny:** ☐

"O Lord, thou hast searched me, and known me. Thou knowest my downsitting and mine uprising, thou understandest my thought afar off. Thou compassest my path and my lying down, and art acquainted with all my ways." - Psalm 139:1-3.

| *Testimonials* |

I have come unto the Father as a 'little child' (been born again). _____ Yes _____ No

I have renewed MY mind. (Changed my way of thinking; 'crucified' MY flesh) _____ Yes _____ No

I live 'one day at a time' (looking to God to supply all of my need). _____ Yes _____ No

I change the things that I can and, the things that I cannot change, I turn over to God (put into His hands). _____ Yes _____ No

Who are YOU in "Christ?" (Explain YOUR relationship to Jesus Christ and YOUR Kingdom ['heavenly'] birthrights):

_____

_____

_____

_____

_____

_____

What road were you on when you met Jesus? (Describe the (1) circumstance or situation that drew YOU to God):

_____

_____

_____

_____

_____

_____

❖ **What are your opinions of these _'prophetic'_ and _'spiritual'_ accounts?**

The report on "Prophecies Received" ("Prophecy of Restoration & Transformation", "Prophecy of God's Calling" and "Prophecy of Business" - their 'future' revelations):

_____

_____

_____

_____

The report "As A Little Child" (Testimony of "coming unto the 'heavenly' Father [spiritually] as a little child."):

_____

_____

_____

_____

What do you have to say <u>overall</u> about "Reflections of Purpose & Destiny" Revealed?

_____

_____

_____

_____

Do you share similar experiences of _"Purpose & Destiny Revealed"_ with the author?...

❖ **Did God reveal 'true' Purpose & Destiny unto you?** _____ Yes _____ No

➤ DO NOT complete this section if YOUR response was 'No'

Did you 'dream dreams' of Purpose & Destiny? _____ Yes _____ No

Did you 'see visions' of Purpose & Destiny? _____ Yes _____ No

Did you receive 'Prophecies' of Purpose & Destiny? _____ Yes _____ No

What is the 'heavenly' Father's (God's) 'Master Plan' for YOU in this earthly realm? (Briefly describe what God has revealed thus far; that which He has 'personally' called you to and the paths He plans for you to take):

Plans:_____

_____

_____

Paths:_____

_____

_____

After coming into revelation of God's 'Master plan' for YOUR life:

How did it make you feel knowing God (your 'heavenly' Father) had a better plan for your life <u>than</u> the life you were presently living? (Explain how you felt on this 'joyous' occasion):

_____

_____

_____

_____

Did you also come into revelation that God had already 'equipped you' to do what it is that He has called you to while living in this earthly realm? (Possess the 'gifts' and 'talents' necessary to walk into your calling) _____ Yes _____ No

When and how did God reveal His 'Purpose & Destiny' for you? (Describe what happened: Were things revealed through dreams and visions, prophecies, the "living word" [Bible], etc?)

_____

_____

_____

_____

❖ **Is YOUR "Joy" full?** (Are you 'spiritually and emotionally' satisfied overall with your life?) _____ Yes _____ No

Respond to (1) of the *following* (2) sections that apply to you:

☐ **MY "Joy" is full:**

Describe what it is that makes your "joy" full: (Walking in God's Purpose; working towards your Destiny? etc.)

_____

_____

_____

_____

_____

Are you a mature, seasoned Christian - full of wisdom; able to discern both good and evil? (Eating the strong meat [solid food] of the word - Hebrews 5:14) _____ Yes _____ No

☐ **MY "Joy"** *is* **_not_** **full:**

Are you continually in search of something? _____ Yes _____ No

If continually in search of something, what it is you seek that YOUR "joy" might be full? (Describe what you think at this time would satisfy your soul's desire: Being 'spiritually and emotionally' satisfied? Walking in Purpose & Destiny?, etc.):

_____

_____

_____

_____

_____

❖ **God is my 'heavenly' Father; I** *do not* **know my Purpose & Destiny:** ☐

Testimonials

I have come unto the Father as "a little child' (been born again). _____ Yes _____ No

I have renewed MY mind (Changed my way of thinking; 'crucified' MY flesh).
_____ Yes _____ No

I live 'one day at a time' (looking to God to supply all of my need). _____ Yes _____ No

Who are YOU in "Christ?" (Explain YOUR relationship to Jesus Christ and YOUR Kingdom ['heavenly'] birthrights):

_____

_____

_____

_____

_____

_____

What road were you on when you met Jesus? (Describe the (1) circumstance or situation that drew YOU to God):

_____

_____

_____

_____

_____

_____

❖ **What are your opinions of these *'prophetic'* and *'spiritual'* accounts:**

The report on "Prophecies Received" ("Prophecy of Restoration & Transformation"; "Prophecy of God's Calling"; and "Prophecy of Business" - their 'future' revelations):

_____

_____

_____

_____

The report "As A Little Child" (Testimony of "coming unto the 'heavenly' Father [spiritually] as a little child"):

_____

_____

_____

_____

What do you have to say <u>overall</u> about "Reflections of Purpose & Destiny" Revealed?

_____

_____

_____

_____

❖ **Do you feel 'spiritually' and 'emotionally' satisfied inside?** _____ Yes _____ No

Are you just coming unto the 'heavenly' Father as "a little child" (in the beginning of knowledge [a 'babe in Christ'] drinking from the 'sincere milk of the word' - Hebrews 5:13)?
_____ Yes _____ No

Are you continually in search of something? _____ Yes _____ No

If <u>continually</u> in search of something - YOUR "Joy" <u>is not</u> full! What is it you seek that YOUR "Joy" might be full? (Describe what you <u>think</u> at this time would satisfy your soul's desire):

_____

_____

_____

_____

_____

❖ **Have you ever asked God to reveal YOUR 'true' Purpose & Destiny unto you?**
(His will, purpose and future for your life) _____ Yes _____ No

Describe in a few words how you <u>think</u> you would feel if you 'perished' due to 'lack of knowledge'... never coming into revelation of who you really were in Christ:

(...**WAIT!** Before you respond, take time out to think about the people who have ... then read Luke 16:19-31; the story of "The rich man and Lazarus.")

_____

_____

"Believe in the Lord your God, so shall ye be established (kept safe); believe his prophets, so shall ye prosper (succeed)." - II Chronicles 20:20.

> ➢ Complete (1) of (2) Main Sections based on YOUR *earlier* response to "Prophecy":

❖ **I believe in the 'gift of Prophecy'** ☐

Testimonials

I believe in Spiritual gifts. _____ Yes _____ No

I believe Spiritual gifts are given to all of God's children. _____ Yes _____ No

I believe God speaks to man through Prophecy. _____ Yes _____ No

Have you ever been given a Prophecy? _____ Yes _____ No

❖ **I *do not* believe in the 'gift of Prophecy':** ☐

Do you believe in 'fruit of the Spirit'? _____ Yes _____ No

Do you believe that you possess certain 'fruit of the Spirit'? _____ Yes _____ No

Do you believe in 'gifts of the Spirit'? _____ Yes _____ No

Do you believe Spiritual gifts are given to all of God's children? _____ Yes _____ No

❖ *If you **believe** in 'Spiritual gifts':* Why is it that you *do not* believe in the particular 'gift of Prophecy'? Explain YOUR predicament:

_____

_____

_____

❖ **"God saith, in the last days He would pour out His Spirit upon all flesh: and sons and daughters shall prophesy" (Acts 2:17 & 18):**

Would you consider 'these days' to be "the last days"? _____ Yes _____ No

Have you ever been given a Prophecy? _____ Yes _____ No

> If you completed "testimonials": You now have YOUR own 'Reflections' of "Jehovah Jireh" - YOUR Provider! (*Genesis 22:14*).
>
> If you <u>did not</u> complete "testimonials": You still have one - given the fact that you have the 'breath of Life' today, "Jehovah Jireh" has been <u>and</u> is YOUR provider!

"For I know the thoughts (plans) that I think toward you, saith the Lord, thoughts (plans) of peace, and not evil, to give you an expected end (future and hope)" - Jeremiah 29:11.

Life's Purpose:

✓ We have been created for God's glory: to praise and worship Him; to walk in love; and to spread the Gospel [The "Good News" of Jesus Christ]. (Ephesians 2:10 and 3:11-21)

✓ Besides coming to repentance (changing our ways) and receiving salvation (being saved), God expects for us to develop our 'Spiritual' gifts and 'natural' talents (blessings) for the uplifting of the Body of Christ; becoming a blessing to others. (John 15:16)

✓ The Bible explains how to live life; it has been written for our life guide. The Book of Proverbs is an excellent place to start for anyone seeking a 'purposeful' life.

Once coming into your 'gifts and talents' [anointing] and you develop them, eventually you will know what things God has personally (purposefully) called you to while living in this earthly realm [Your life's mission]. And if you have been given a 'special' anointing [calling] for work directly inside (or for) the Church, God will reveal it unto you - whether you walk in it or not.

Life's Destiny:

✓ Salvation is the "destiny" of all 'true' believers (John 3:3; Ephesians 1:13-14).

✓ We are created for God's glory: for adoption back into His Kingdom (since the falling away in the Garden of Eden); to inherit the things of God; to live with Him in eternity. (Galatians 4:5, Colossians 3:4.)

✓ Major parts of our life's destiny - of which we DO NOT have control - have already been predestined. They include our birth, our families, unexpected events in life, and death.

✓ Then, there are certain parts of life's destiny - of which we DO have control - that is predestined on how we chose to live life. These certain parts of life's destiny are due to 'cause and effect' [based on the choices we make in life]. Things happen in life at times not because we are not saved, but because of the things we do that <u>are not</u> according to 'laws of the Spirit'.

✓ Living by God's will ['Master' Plan] brings 'true' Purpose & Destiny; known as being 'justified by faith'.

✓ Some people were *"predestined"* (*born*) for the Kingdom of God (Jeremiah 1:5, Matthew 1:18-25); and others have been *"adopted"* into the Kingdom of God by faith (Hebrews 11).

✓ Meditate on the Law; Psalm 119:1-176 is an excellent place to start for seeking salvation.

"And we know all things work together for good to them who love God, to them who are the called according to his purpose." Romans 8:28.

"Moreover whom he did predestinate, them he also called: and whom he called, them he also justified: and whom he justified, them he also glorified." - Romans 8:30.

Chapter Reflections: (Write additional thoughts/feelings about this Chapter here:)

_____

_____

_____

_____

_____

_____

Chapter 5

Heavenly Treasures

$\mathcal{I}$s there really a "pot of gold" at the end of the rainbow in the sky?

Many people seem to choose the "practical" way of living (will of the flesh) rather than the "spiritual" way of living (will of God). The "practical" way of living will cause people to lose out on that precious "pot of gold" ["heavenly treasures"] at the end of the rainbow in the sky; which contains life's most greatest treasures - "prosperity" - the true riches of life.

My Reflections:

I am a 'child of God.' _____ Yes _____ No

I have embraced God's 'mutual' promises. (Promises made to all of His children) _____ Yes _____ No

I believe in "Heavenly Treasures." _____ Yes _____ No

I have been blessed with "Spiritual blessings."_____ Yes _____ No

I have been blessed with "Gifts of the Spirit." _____ Yes _____ No

I have been blessed with "Fruit of the Spirit." _____ Yes _____ No

I walk 'in Spirit and in Truth.' _____ Yes _____ No

☐ I live by the "law of the Spirit."
☐ I live the "Practical" Way.

❖ **I live by the "law of the Spirit":** ☐

"Ye are of God, little children, and have overcome them: because greater is he that is in you, than he that is in the world." - I John 4:4

Testimonials

I have renewed my mind. _____ Yes_____ No

I 'fear' [reverence] God. _____ Yes_____ No

I am a 'child of God.' _____ Yes_____ No

I know that I am 'spirit.' _____ Yes_____ No

The Holy Spirit dwells within me. _____ Yes_____ No

What do you have to say <u>overall</u> about "Reflections of Heavenly Treasures?" (Express your feelings concerning these 'spiritual' blessings and gifts):

_____

_____

_____

_____

Have you considered (thought about) the author's theory on "the pot of gold" at the end of the rainbow in the sky? _____ Yes_____ No

Have you been blessed with 'Heavenly Treasures' (Spiritual blessings, gifts and fruit of the Spirit)? _____ Yes_____ No

Is it evident you walk "in Spirit and in Truth?" (Being transparent - hiding nothing; bearing 'righteous' fruit and possessing 'spiritual' characteristics) _____ Yes_____ No

Do you have family and friends you sometimes wonder "who might their real father be?" _____ Yes_____ No

Do you have family and friends whom you have separated yourself from (come out from among) since being 'born' again? _____ Yes_____ No

If you <u>have</u> family and friends you sometimes wonder "who might their real father be" or have separated yourself from, have you ever ministered to them? _____ Yes_____ No

❖ I live the "Practical" Way: ☐

"But without faith, it is impossible to please him; for he that cometh to God must believe that he is, and that he is a rewarder of them that diligently seek him." - Hebrews 11:6

Testimonials

Do you 'fear' [reverence] God? _____ Yes_____ No

Are you a 'child of God'? (Have you been 'born' again?) _____ Yes_____ No

Has God revealed Himself to you? _____ Yes_____ No

Do you believe that you are 'spirit'? _____ Yes_____ No

Does the Holy Spirit dwell within you? _____ Yes_____ No

What do you have to say <u>overall</u> about "Reflections of Heavenly Treasures?" (Express your feelings concerning these 'spiritual' blessings and 'spiritual' gifts):

_____

_____

_____

_____

Have you considered (thought about) the author's theory on the "pot of gold" at the end of the rainbow in the sky? _____ Yes_____ No

Have you been blessed with Heavenly Treasures (Spiritual blessings, gifts and fruit of the Spirit)? _____ Yes_____ No

Do you proclaim to be 'a child of God'? _____ Yes_____ No

If you <u>proclaim</u> to be a 'child of God':

And you fear [reverence] God <u>and</u> the Holy Spirit dwells in you: Why are you living the "practical" way? [Explain YOUR predicament]:

_____

_____

_____

_____

Could you be suffering from "failure to thrive?" (Lack of 'spiritual' nourishment)
_____ Yes_____ No

Have you failed to renew YOUR mind - condition yourself to live by 'laws of the Spirit'? (Romans 7:25; 12:2 and Ephesians 4:23 & 24) _____ Yes_____ No

If you *have* failed to renew YOUR mind:

Are you willing to change YOUR way of thinking and living (receive a new "mindset") to come into the things (blessings) God wills for you? _____ Yes_____ No

Living the 'practical' way separates one from God:

- In order to come into the promises of God (to live an abundant life), one must totally submit to the 'Holy Spirit'; thereby, operating (living) by 'laws of the Spirit'.

- Meditate on the Law - Psalms 119:1-176 would be an excellent place to start.

Reflections of Heavenly Treasures:

> If you completed "testimonials": You now have *YOUR* own 'Reflections' of "El-Shaddai" - the Almighty God (*Genesis 17:1*) showing His compassion & love for you!

Heavenly Treasures [Kingdom Birthrights]: Heavenly Treasures are also [earthly benefits] (James 1:17). After being born again we are adopted into a new family - the Kingdom of God - becoming heirs of 'Kingdom' benefits while living in this earthly realm. We DO NOT have to wait until 'the end time' to become receivers of these inheritances.

As children of God we have fellowship with Him and access to Him. We have also been provided guidance and protection by Him - through comfort from the Holy Spirit and his angels. Some of these other "Heavenly Treasures" (earthly birthrights; benefits) include:

- Gifts of the Holy Spirit
- An abundant [prosperous] life
- Deliverance and healing
- Dominion [power and authority]
- Release from enemy strongholds

Following are Scriptures describing 'heavenly treasures' (our 'Kingdom' birthrights): Deuteronomy 28:1-14; Psalms 68:19 and 103:2-17; Matthew 6:19-21; Titus 3:4-7.

Laws of God: Study and meditate on these laws of God to show thyself approved:

- The **'Spiritual'** law (The first and great commandment) - *Matthew 22:37-38*
- The **'Physical'** law (The law of nature) - *Genesis 8:22* and *Colossians 1:17*
- The **'Moral'** law (The perfect law of liberty) - *James 1:25* and *II Timothy 3:17*
- The **'Social'** law (The royal law) - *James 2:8* and *Matthew 22:39*

[Keep this in remembrance: The law (works we do) has <u>never</u> saved anyone. We are saved by God's grace - through 'saving' faith (belief in Jesus Christ, the redemptive works of the cross; belief in God and walking in His ways. Known as being "justified by faith" - James 2:20-26).]

Chapter Reflections: (Write additional thoughts/feelings about this Chapter here:)

_____

_____

_____

_____

_____

_____

Chapter 6

Spiritual Awakenings

Not everyone has "20/20" Vision - There are some things we can all see, and some things only a few of us can see.

Nor does everyone have perfect hearing. *"Faith comes by hearing, and hearing by the word of God"* (Romans 10:17).

"Therefore speak I to them in parables: because they seeing see not; and hearing they hear not, neither do they understand." - Matthew 13:13.

"And it shall come to pass in the last days, saith God, I will pour out of my Spirit upon all flesh: and your sons and your daughters shall prophesy, and your young men shall see visions, and your old men shall dream dreams: - Acts 2:17

And on my servants and on my handmaidens I will pour out in those days of my Spirit; and they shall prophesy:" - Acts 2:18

My Reflections:

I have "eyes to see" (both levels of vision). _____ Yes _____ No

I have "ears to hear" (live by Faith). _____ Yes _____ No

I have dreamed 'mystical' dreams and/or visions. _____ Yes _____ No

I am fully persuaded God has poured out His Spirit upon all flesh. _____ Yes _____ No

☐   I have 'Reflections of Spiritual Awakenings'.

☐   I <u>do not</u> have 'Reflections on Spiritual Awakenings'.

> ➤ Complete (1) of (2) Main Sections based on YOUR response to "Spiritual Awakening."

❖ **I have 'Reflections of Spiritual Awakenings':** ☐

Testimonials

I believe the theory that "babies and little children can see things that adults cannot see" is: _____ Fact _____ Fiction

❖ **What are your theories of these _'mystical'_ and _'supernatural'_ accounts?**

The reports on "The Leprechauns" and "The Fairy God Mother" (These 'mystical' accounts of ability to see these things in the natural realm - remember the author was not alone) :

_____

_____

_____

_____

The report on "Grandmother's Visit" (This detailed 'mystical' account of ability to see [and describe] a person from the past in the natural realm):

_____

_____

_____

_____

The report on 'The Vision of the Ram' (The vision, revelation and manifestation of healing):

_____

_____

_____

_____

Express your <u>overall</u> opinion on "Reflections of Spiritual Awakenings":

_____

_____

_____

_____

Do you believe the author's reports of 'Spiritual Awakenings'? (In the things the author has seen)
_____ Yes _____ No

Do you share similar experiences of _'Spiritual Awakenings'_ with the author?...

❖ **Did you see things as a child?** _____ Yes _____ No

➢ DO NOT complete this section if YOUR response was **'No'**

What types of things did you see? (Describe at least (2) accounts of what it was or who it was you saw in the 'supernatural' - in a dream or in a vision):

1. _____

    _____

2. _____

    _____

Did you see things that 'scared/frightened' you? _____ Yes _____ No

Did you see things that 'excited/surprised' you? _____ Yes _____ No

When you saw these things, did any of these things remind you of a 'fairy tale'?
_____ Yes _____ No

Were you by yourself when you saw these things? _____ Yes _____ No

Did you tell anyone when you saw these things? _____ Yes _____ No

If you <u>told</u> someone, did they believe YOUR story? _____ Yes _____ No

❖ **Have you seen things as an adult?** _____ Yes _____ No

➢ DO NOT complete this section if YOUR response was **'No'**

I have seen things that 'scared/frightened' me. _____ Yes _____ No

I have seen things that 'excited/surprised' me. _____ Yes _____ No

I have seen things that reminded me of 'fairy tales'. _____ Yes _____ No

What types of things have you seen? (Describe at least (2) accounts: what it was or who it was you saw in the 'supernatural' that led to 'a spiritual awakening'):

1. _____

_____

2. _____

_____

Were you able to determine their meanings (understood what it meant)? _____ Yes _____ No

If <u>unable</u> to determine their meaning, have you asked God to reveal these things to you?
_____ Yes _____ No

Did you tell anyone when you saw these things? _____ Yes _____ No

If you <u>told</u> someone, did they believe YOUR story? _____ Yes_____ No

If they <u>did not</u> believe YOUR story, briefly describe how this made you feel:

_____

_____

[**Note:** This is why it is not a good idea to tell everything that you see or hear. There are certain things that God will reveal to you that He wants you to keep to yourself; some things are only for you. And those things that He does want you to reveal, He will place within your spirit (and you will sense) when the time is right for you to reveal it.]

Do you see things often? _____ Yes _____ No

Do you believe God speaks to man through dreams and visions? _____ Yes _____ No

Have you ever dreamed a 'mystical' dream or seen a 'mystical' vision? (See something strange or out of the ordinary while asleep or awake that you thought may have had meaning?)
_____ Yes _____ No

Do you believe you have been blessed with "eyes to see" and "ears to hear?" _____ Yes _____ No

❖ **I *do not* have 'Reflections on Spiritual Awakenings':** ☐

I believe the theory that "babies and little children can see things that adults cannot see" is:
_____ Fact _____ Fiction

❖ **What are your theories of these *'mystical' and supernatural'* accounts:**

The reports on "The Leprechauns" and "The Fairy God Mother" (These 'mystical' accounts of ability to see these things in the natural realm - remember the author was not alone):

_____

_____

_____

_____

The report on "Grandmother's Visit" (This detailed 'mystical' account of ability to see [and describe] a person from the past in the natural realm):

_____

_____

_____

_____

The report on "The Vision of the Ram" (The vision, revelation and manifestation of healing):

_____

_____

_____

_____

Express your <u>overall</u> opinion on "Reflections of Spiritual Awakenings" :

_____

_____

_____

_____

Do you believe God speaks to man through dreams and visions? _____ Yes _____ No

Do you desire to be blessed with "eyes to see" and "ears to hear" ["20/20" Vision]
_____ Yes _____ No

Do you believe the author's reports of 'Spiritual Awakenings'? _____ Yes _____ No

❖ **Do you recall seeing things as a child?** _____ Yes _____ No

❖ **Have you ever seen things as an adult?** _____ Yes _____ No

> ➢ DO NOT complete this section if **both** responses were **'No'**

If you have seen things as a child or an adult:

Describe some of these things that you have seen: (What it was or who it was you saw in the supernatural - in a dream or in a vision - that _may_ have been a "spiritual awakening.")

1. _____

_____

2. _____

_____

3. _____

_____

4. _____

_____

Reflections of Spiritual Awakenings:

If you completed "testimonials": You now have YOUR own 'Reflections' of "El-Shaddai" - the Almighty God (*Genesis 17:1*) unveiling 'Mysteries (hidden truths) of the Kingdom of Heaven' unto you!

Chapter Reflections: (Write additional thoughts/feelings about this Chapter here:)

_____

_____

_____

_____

_____

_____

Chapter 7

Spiritual Nurturing

Counselor, comforter, protector, mediator... these are only a few of the many faces (attributes) of the "heavenly Father" (God). They are measures of "spiritual nurturing" He provides for His children; through His son - Jesus Christ; the 'Bread of Life.' [John 6:35].

"Spiritual nurturing" (received from remaining part of the vine - *John 15*) will sustain one's faith to the point that "it shall never waiver."

My Reflections:

I believe in the life-changing, supernatural, powerful 'name of Jesus.' _____ Yes _____ No

I believe God is "all powerful" (He is 'omnipotent'). _____ Yes _____ No

I believe God is "all knowing" (He is 'omniscient'). _____ Yes _____ No

I believe God is "everywhere" (He is 'omnipresent'). _____ Yes _____ No

I have prayed 'prayers of repentance' to God. _____ Yes _____ No

I have been 'comforted' by the Holy Spirit. _____ Yes _____ No

I have received measures of 'Spiritual Nurturing'. _____ Yes _____ No

☐ I have 'Reflections of Spiritual Nurturing'.

☐ I <u>do not</u> have 'Reflections on Spiritual Nurturing'.

> Complete (1) of (2) Main Sections based on YOUR response to "Spiritual Nurturing."

❖ I have 'Reflections of Spiritual Nurturing': ☐

Testimonials

Have you ever committed a 'sin' against yourself? _____ Yes _____ No

Have you ever committed a 'sin' against God? _____ Yes _____ No

Have you repented and have been 'set free' from these sins? _____ Yes _____ No

Have you ever felt the 'supernatural' power of the Holy Spirit? _____ Yes _____ No

I know what it feels like to be 'resurrected' (born again). _____ Yes _____ No

I have prayers that have been answered. _____ Yes _____ No

I have received 'admonishment' (teaching, correction, direction, and love) from the Holy Spirit. _____ Yes _____ No

My faith [belief] in God is sustaining; it shall never waiver. _____ Yes _____ No

God is _____ to me! (Filling in the blanks below, express how you really feel about God):

_____

_____

_____

'Reflect' on (list) a few times when God has shown His face to you: (When you were brokenhearted and disappointed within; when you were comforted by the presence of the Holy Spirit; when a way was made for you out of no way, etc.)

1_____

2_____

3_____

4_____

Do you believe a place has been prepared 'specifically' for you in the Kingdom of heaven? _____ Yes; I am fully persuaded; _____ Not Sure [Uncertain]

If fully persuaded a place has been prepared for you, explain why you are so confident:

_____

_____

_____

_____

❖ **What are your opinions of these accounts on *'spiritual'* nurturing?**

The report on 'God's Covenants' (The "Dream of the Tongue" and "Vision of Covenants" [hearing God's spiritual voice] and their revelations):

_____

_____

_____

_____

The report on 'God's Love' ("Affirmations from God"; the unction [urgings] of the 'Holy Spirit' and comfort from revelations revealed):

_____

_____

_____

_____

The report on 'God's Comfort' (The "Comforter of the Holy Spirit" [being held, hearing the spiritual voice and what was said] and its revelation):

_____

_____

_____

_____

What do you have to say <u>overall</u> about "Reflections of Spiritual Nurturing?"

_____

_____

_____

_____

Do you believe the author's reports of 'Spiritual Nurturing'? _____ Yes _____ No

Do you share similar experiences of *'Spiritual Nurturing'* with the author?...

❖ **Do you receive daily measures of 'Spiritual Nurturing'?** _____ Yes _____ No

> ➢ DO NOT complete this section if YOUR response was **'No'**

How does God nurture you daily? (What takes place in your life daily whereby you know you are part of the vine? Are you being comforted; providing for; protected; shown favor?)

_____

_____

_____

_____

Express how it feels knowing the one and only, 'true and living' God loves and nurtures you:

_____

_____

_____

Have you ever experienced "a peace that passeth all understanding"? (Received a visit from the "Comforter of the Holy Spirit") _____ Yes _____ No

❖ **Have you ever made Covenants [Vows] to God?** _____ Yes _____ No _____ Not Sure

"Better is it that thou shouldest not to vow, than that thou shouldest vow and not pay." - Ecclesiastes 5:5

Have you ever prayed to God to get you out of a 'negative' predicament (due to your actions) promising to never get involved in a predicament like that again? _____ Yes _____ No

Have you ever prayed to God <u>after</u> committing an immoral, corrupt, or dishonest act promising never to commit this act again? _____ Yes _____ No

Have you ever 'deliberately' prayed to God <u>before</u> committing an immoral, corrupt, or dishonest act, promising to never commit this act again? _____ Yes _____ No

[**Note:** If you answered **"Yes"** to <u>any</u> question, you have made a "Covenant to God"].

If you <u>have</u> made 'Covenants to God' <u>AND</u> broke these Covenants:

Do you now understand that 'Promises to God' are 'Covenants to God?' _____ Yes _____ No

Did you feel convicted (guilty) after breaking your 'Promise(s) to God? _____ Yes _____ No

If you 'knowingly' committed an immoral, corrupt, or dishonest act, did you feel convicted (guilty) after <u>deliberately</u> trying to compromise with God? _____ Yes _____ No

Have you repented and been 'set free' from these sins? _____ Yes _____ No

Do you often ask God for forgiveness, and repent, of things you 'unconsciously' do - trespasses due to human nature - that may have offended the 'heavenly' Father or others. _____ Yes _____ No

❖ **Have you ever heard a *'spiritual'* voice?** _____ Yes_____ No_____ Not Sure

Have you ever heard your name called out loud in the voice of someone you knew and, when you responded, they stated that they did not call your name? _____ Yes_____ No

Have you ever been alone and heard your name whispered softly in a voice you did not know... realizing "no one" was physically there? _____ Yes_____ No

> ➢ DO NOT complete this section if **_both_** responses to the **last (2)** questions were **'No'**

- Remember the Lord called Samuel (3) times before he answered; hearing the call, but did not recognize the voice, assuming it was Eli the priest. But this was before Samuel knew the Lord. (*I Samuel 3:4-10*).

- God's children know His voice and other 'heavenly' [messengers] voices they hear. (*John 10:3 & 4*). If you hear any other voices - flee from (rebuke) them; they may be demonic, [ungodly] voices. (*John 10:5*).

Do you hear 'spiritual' voices often? _____ Yes_____ No

Are these 'spiritual' voices ['heavenly'] voices that you hear (have heard)?_____ Yes_____ No

If you <u>have</u> heard 'heavenly' voices:

Have any of the voices you heard ever asked you to do anything? _____ Yes_____ No

If a 'heavenly' voice <u>has asked</u> you to do something:

What did the voice ask you to do? (Briefly describe what was asked of you:)

_____

_____

_____

Did you follow through on what was asked of you? _____ Yes_____ No

If you <u>did not</u> follow through on what was asked of you, briefly explain why? (Was it because you found it too impossible to believe; ignored what you heard; lacked faith in ability to follow through, etc.):

_____

_____

_____

_____

Do you believe that you have heard God's 'heavenly' voice? _____ Yes_____ No

If you believe you <u>have</u> heard God's 'heavenly' voice:

How do you know it was God's voice that you heard? (Are you familiar with His voice? Was anything in particular said to you?)

_____

_____

_____

What has God said to you or asked you to do? (What did He reveal?)

_____

_____

_____

_____

Did you speak (talk) to God when He spoke to you? _____ Yes_____ No

Have you ever questioned God about your life? _____ Yes_____ No

When was the last time you heard God's 'spiritual' voice? _____

(*"Every one that is of the truth heareth [understands] my voice"* - John 18:37.)

❖ **Have you ever dreamed a 'mystical' (*'spiritual'*) dream?** _____Yes _____ No

❖ **Have you ever seen a 'mystical' (*'spiritual'*) vision?** _____ Yes _____ No

> ➢ DO NOT complete the [following] *last* section if **both** responses were 'No'

Do you believe your 'mystical' dream(s) or vision(s) may have had spiritual meaning concerning your purpose or destiny? _____ Yes _____ No

Do you believe these dreams and/or visions were from God? _____ Yes _____ No

Do you dream these dreams and/or see these visions often? _____ Yes _____ No

Do (did) you understand these dreams and/or visions? _____ Yes _____ No

If you <u>do not</u> (did not) understand these dreams and/or visions, have you ever asked God to reveal their meanings to you? _____ Yes _____ No

In any of these dreams and/or visions, did you hear a 'spiritual' voice? _____ Yes _____ No

Did you record [write down] any of these dreams or visions (what was said to you, what you heard, and/or what you saw)? _____ Yes _____ No

'Reflect' on at least one (1) of these 'mystical' dreams or visions of God showing Himself (His face) to you. (Briefly describe what took place and what you saw or heard:)

_____

_____

_____

_____

_____

If you <u>understood</u> at least one (1) of these 'mystical' dreams or visions, what did or was God revealing to you?

_____

_____

_____

"But blessed are your eyes, for they see: and your ears, for they hear. For verily I say unto you, That many prophets and righteous men have desired to see those things which ye see, and have not seen them; and to hear those things which you hear and have not heard them. Hear ye therefore the "parable of the sower." - Matthew 13:16-18.

❖ **I *do not* have 'Reflections on Spiritual Nurturing':** ☐

Have you ever committed a 'sin' against yourself? _____ Yes _____ No

Have you ever committed a 'sin' against God? _____ Yes _____ No

Have you ever made 'promises to God' and broke them? _____ Yes _____ No

Have you ever tried compromising with God? _____ Yes _____ No

If you __have__ done any of the above things:

Have you ever felt guilty? _____ Yes _____ No

Have you ever repented and been 'set free' from this (these) things? _____ Yes _____ No

If you have not repented, briefly explain "why":

_____

_____

_____

[**Reminder:** *"He that covereth his sins shall not prosper: but whoso confesseth and forsaketh them shall have mercy"* - Proverb 28:13.]

Do you believe that God "sees all" and "hears all"? _____ Yes _____ No

❖ **Have you ever made Covenants [Vows] to God?** _____ Yes _____ No _____ Not Sure

   "Better is it that thou shouldest not to vow, than that thou shouldest vow and not pay." - Ecclesiastes 5:5

Have you ever prayed to God to get out of a 'negative' predicament (due to your actions) promising never to get involved in a predicament like that again? _____ Yes _____ No

Have you ever prayed to God <u>after</u> committing an immoral, corrupt, or dishonest act promising never to commit this act again? _____ Yes _____ No

Have you ever 'deliberately' prayed to God <u>before</u> committing an immoral, corrupt, or dishonest act, promising to never commit this act again? _____ Yes _____ No

[**Note:** If you answered **"Yes"** to <u>any</u> question, you have made a "Covenant to God"].

If you __have__ made 'Covenants to God' __AND__ broke these Covenants:

Do you now understand that 'Promises to God' are 'Covenants to God?' _____ Yes _____ No

Did you feel guilty after breaking your 'Promise(s) to God? _____ Yes _____ No

If you 'knowingly' committed an immoral, corrupt, or dishonest act, did you feel guilty after <u>deliberately</u> trying to compromise with God? _____ Yes _____ No

Do you often ask God for forgiveness (and repent) of things you 'unconsciously' do - trespasses due to human nature - that may have offended the 'heavenly' Father or others. _____ Yes _____ No

Have you ever experienced a "peace that passeth all understanding"? (Peace 'within' at a time when ordinarily you should have felt differently 'inside'?) _____ Yes_____ No

❖ **Do you have 'Reflections' of life in the 'Valley of Dry Bones'?** _____ Yes_____ No

If you have 'Reflections of life in the Valley of Dry Bones' and have come out from that place, would you consider this experience to have been 'Spiritual nurturing'? _____ Yes_____ No

Do you wind up in the same predicaments over and over again? _____ Yes_____ No

Is your life 'out of order' (in disarray; a mess)? _____ Yes_____ No

If your life is 'out of order'; or you do not have 'peace' within: Do you know (understand) why? _____ Yes_____ No

Are you taking your precious 'gift of life' for granted? _____ Yes_____ No

Do you believe in the life-changing, supernatural, powerful 'name of Jesus'? _____ Yes_____ No

If you believe in the 'name of Jesus' are you willing to ask the Lord to bless you and open your eyes so you can proclaim 'works of nurturing' in your life? _____ Yes_____ No

❖ **Do you believe a place has been prepared for you in the 'Kingdom of Heaven'?**
_____ Yes_____ Not Sure [Uncertain]

If you are uncertain (not sure) a place has been prepared for you in the 'Kingdom of heaven', briefly explain why you do not feel worthy of what has been prepared for you (John 14:2-3):

_____

_____

_____

_____

Do you believe that God is a 'God of many chances'? _____ Yes_____ No

Do you believe 'whom the Lord loveth he correcteth' (Proverb 3:12)? _____ Yes_____ No

God is _____ to me! (Filling in the 'following' blanks, express how you really feel about God)

[Remember: Be 'honest' with your inner-self. This is the only way you will be 'set free' from the bondages in YOUR thinking. And although God already knows how you feel inside, He is the only one that can release you to "be who it is He has called you to be!"]

_____

_____

_____

_____

❖ **What are your opinions of these accounts on *'spiritual'* nurturing?**

The report on 'God's Covenants' (The "Dream of the Tongue" and "Vision of Covenants" [hearing God's spiritual voice] and their revelations):

_____

_____

_____

_____

The report on 'God's Love' ("Affirmations from God"; unction [urgings] of the 'Holy Spirit' and comfort from revelations revealed):

_____

_____

_____

_____

The report on 'God's Comfort' (The "Comforter of the Holy Spirit" [being held, hearing the spiritual voice, and what was said] and its revelation):

_____

_____

_____

_____

What do you have to say <u>overall</u> about "Reflections of Spiritual Nurturing?"

_____

_____

_____

_____

Do you believe these reports of 'Spiritual Nurturing'? _____ Yes _____ No

❖ **Are you proclaiming a personal *[covenant]* relationship with God?** _____ Yes _____ No

> ➤ Complete this section **ONLY** if YOUR response was **'Yes'**

If proclaiming a personal [covenant] relationship with God, how is it that you <u>do not</u> feel Spiritual Nurturing (daily comfort, provision, and protection)? [What have you missed?...]

Explain YOUR predicament:

_____

_____

_____

_____

Do you suppose that you could be suffering from "failure to thrive"? (Lacking 'spiritual nourishment' (victory) in the natural [world]) _____ Yes _____ No

Do you lack knowledge and understanding in this area? _____ Yes _____ No

"All the ways of a man are clean in his own eyes; but the Lord weigheth the spirits [motives; heart]." - Proverb 16:2

[Remember: The "Lord's Prayer" (Matthew 6:9-13) and the author's "Vision of Covenants"; one must repent from sin (trespasses) on a regular basis in order to live prosperous. This is one reason why 'Jesus' prayed to the Father to "forgive us of the things that we know not what we do" (Luke 23:34). Meditate on Psalm 51.]

❖ **Have you ever heard a *'spiritual'* voice?** _____ Yes _____ No _____ Not Sure

Have you ever heard your name called out loud in the voice of someone you knew and, when you responded, they stated that they did not call your name? _____ Yes _____ No

Have you ever been alone and heard your name whispered softly in a voice that you did not know... realizing "no one" was physically there? _____ Yes _____ No

- Remember the Lord called Samuel (3) times before he answered; hearing the call, but did not recognize the voice, assuming it was Eli the priest. But this was before Samuel knew the Lord. (*I Samuel 3:4-10*).

- God's children know His voice and any other 'heavenly' (messengers) voices they hear. (*John 10:3 & 4*). If you hear any other spiritual voices - flee from [rebuke] them; they may be demonic, [ungodly] voices. (*John 10:5*).

> ➢ Respond to (1) of the following (3) sections that apply to you.

☐ **I have heard *'spiritual'* voices:**

Do you hear 'spiritual' voices often? _____ Yes_____ No

Are these 'spiritual' voices 'heavenly' voices that you hear (have heard)?_____ Yes_____ No

Do you believe that you have heard God's 'heavenly' voice? _____ Yes_____ No

Have any of the 'heavenly' spiritual voices you have heard ever asked you to do anything? _____ Yes_____ No

If a 'heavenly' spiritual voice <u>has asked</u> you to do anything:

What did the voice ask you to do? (Briefly describe what was asked of you):

_____

_____

_____

Did you follow through on what was asked of you? _____ Yes_____ No

If you <u>did not</u> follow through, briefly explain why? (Was it because you found it too impossible to believe; ignored what you heard; lacked faith in ability to follow through, etc.):

_____

_____

☐ **I have *<u>never</u>* heard a 'spiritual' voice:**

☐ **I am *<u>not sure</u>* if I have heard a 'spiritual' voice:**

- Let me make mention again that even though we are all God's children, we all have a different [individual] relationship with Him. So for some of you, this does not mean that God has never spoken to you, only that you have not developed an 'ear to hear' His voice.

- Then too, many of God's children have never heard His voice; led to believe that He no longer speaks to His children. If you have professed (believe) that you <u>cannot</u> hear God's voice - you have turned a 'deaf' ear, and this is why you have not heard His 'extraordinary' voice. You are not walking in all of His 'promises'! [John 10:1-4; 18:37].

"Behold, I stand at the door, and knock: if any man hear my voice, and open the door, I will come into him" - Revelation 3:20.

❖ **Have you ever dreamed a *'mystical'* dream?** _____ Yes _____ No _____ Not Sure

❖ **Have you ever seen a *'mystical'* vision?** _____ Yes _____ No_____ Not Sure

> ➤ Respond to (1) of the ***following*** (3) sections that apply to you.

☐ **I have experienced a *'mystical'* dream and/or vision:**

Testimonials

Did you write these dreams and/or visions down? _____ Yes _____ No

Have you ever seen a vision (while asleep or awake) that may have had 'spiritual' meaning concerning your life's purpose or destiny? _____ Yes _____ No

Have you ever asked God to reveal the meaning of these dreams and/or visions to you? _____ Yes _____ No

Do you believe these dreams and/or visions could eventually evolve into "Dreams Fulfilled"? _____ Yes _____ No

[**Note**: Start keeping a 'spiritual' journal. The 'heavenly' Father (God) may be speaking to you; wanting to bless you and direct YOUR path to 'true' Purpose & Destiny - His 'will' for your life. *Job 33:14-18*].

☐ **I have *never* experienced a *'mystical'* dream or vision:**

☐ **I am *not sure* if I have experienced a *'mystical'* dream or vision:**

*If you have **never** or, are **not sure** you have; experienced a 'mystical' dream or vision:*

- You probably do not remember or, did not/do not have "eyes to see."

- Many "Mysteries (hidden truths) of the Kingdom of Heaven" are unveiled to man through dreams and visions. The 'spirit man' never sleeps - only the 'physical (natural) body' of man sleeps (rests).

- The Bible contains many books (stories) on dreams and visions from God.

- Case studies have also proved that man dreams (visualizes) every night while sleeping.

> If you completed "testimonials": You now have YOUR own 'Reflections' of "Jehovah-Shalom" - the Prince (Lord) of Peace that comforts thee. (*Judges 6:24*)

Sin: We have all committed sin(s) against God and sin(s) against ourselves one time or another. We have all missed the mark (James 2:10). No man is perfect, no, not one!

God's Nurturing: These Scriptures reveal some of God's many faces (attributes) of love: Jeremiah 31:9; Psalm 68:5; Matthew 7:7; and Romans 8:15.

'Blessings' through courses of Dreams and Visions: These Scriptures reveal 'blessings' of 'true' Purpose & Destiny given by God to His people through dreams and visions: Genesis 31:11-13; I Kings 3:5-15; Job: 33:14-18; and Matthew 1:20-25.

Christians suffering from "Failure to Thrive": These are "babes in Christ" [Hebrews 5:12-13] who have failed to 'spiritually' develop into "mature (full-grown) Christians" [Hebrews 5:41]. Many Christians, after being saved, continue living the "practical way" trying to fit God into their lives, instead of living by "laws of the Spirit." This can also be described as a "carnal mentality."

Then, many are not walking in (believing, acting upon) all of God's promises [lack in faith]. The Word of God states, "Whom shall he teach knowledge? And whom shall he make to understand doctrine? them that are weaned from the milk, and drawn from the breasts." ..."For precept must be upon precept, line upon line... here a little, and there a little" - *Isaiah 28:9-10*.

Spiritual Voices: There are two (2) types of 'spiritual' voices: 1) 'Heavenly' voices; and 2) 'demonic' voices. Learn the difference between the two (2).

✓ If you have heard your name called out loud in the voice of someone you knew and they did not call your name: God will sometimes speak to His children in a familiar voice - in order to get their attention - because they do not recognize His voice.

✓ Once fully coming unto the 'heavenly' Father "as a little child," you will eventually develop revelation [discernment] of knowing God's voice when you hear it (having "ears to hear"). [*"Everyone that is of the truth heareth my voice"* - John 18:37.]

Chapter Reflections: (Write additional thoughts/feelings about this Chapter here:)

_____

_____

_____

_____

_____

_____

Chapter 8

Spiritual Warnings

After drawing near to God, He will redirect your path; right in the middle of a road - just when you are apt to making another wrong turn. (When you failed to stop at "stop signs" or yield at "warning signs" vividly posted).

God will purposefully intervene in YOUR various relationships to warn you and protect you from further endurance of hurt and pain.

"Thou hast hidden these things from the wise and prudent, and hast revealed them unto babes." - Matthew 11:25; Luke 10:21.

My Reflections:

I understand that I am 'spirit.' _____ Yes _____ No

I believe God gives warnings to protect His children. _____ Yes _____ No

I believe God gives warnings against 'negative' relationships. _____ Yes _____ No

I believe God gives warnings through dreams and visions. _____ Yes _____ No

I have experienced tormenting nightmares. _____ Yes _____ No

I believe in the gift of 'Spiritual Warfare'. _____ Yes _____ No

☐ I have 'Reflections of Spiritual Warnings'.
☐ I do not have 'Reflections on Spiritual Warnings'.

❖ **I have 'Reflections of Spiritual Warnings':** ☐

Testimonials

I know that I am 'spirit'. _____ Yes _____ No

God has warned me and protected me. _____ Yes _____ No

I believe in 'Spiritual Attacks'. _____ Yes _____ No

Have you ever thought about going somewhere or doing something and a 'negative' feeling (bad vibe) came over you? _____ Yes_____ No

If you <u>have</u> sensed this feeling (whether you went or not), did something 'negative or bad' happen? _____ Yes_____ No

Have you ever planned to be somewhere on time, ending up running behind schedule, and on the road you were traveling or at the place of destination, a 'life-threatening' incident occurred just before your arrival? _____ Yes_____ No

If you have <u>had</u> this experience, did you consider the fact that if you were on schedule you could have been involved in the 'life-threatening' incident that occurred? _____ Yes_____ No

[**_Note:_** If you have had any of these experiences, know that it was God warning or protecting you. You never know 'who' or 'what' God may have been protecting (saving) you from].

❖ **Has God ever 'divinely' intervened at the beginning of a relationship or friendship... giving you the first subtle, warning sign when:**

   1. After being introduced to the person, you felt a bad vibe? _____ Yes_____ No

   2. In public with this person for the first time, they said something or did something and you sensed in your heart [spirit] it was not the right thing to say or do? _____ Yes_____ No

[**_Note:_** If you have had <u>any</u> of these experiences and ignored God's early warning signs to protect you, be watchful. This is how we wind up with someone 'out of the will of God' in our life - that could eventually lead to living in the 'Valley of Dry Bones'.]

If you have <u>had</u> any of these experiences and ignored them, did you learn from them? _____ Yes_____ No

❖ **What do you think about the [following] _'spiritual'_ and _'mystical'_ accounts?**

The report on the "Vision of Spiritual Warfare" (Hearing the 'spiritual' voice, seeing the vision of warfare, and its revelation):

_____

_____

_____

_____

The report on the "Dream of the Ring" (This 'mystical' dream, its revelations, interpretations and manifestation of 'deceitfulness' coming to pass):

_____

_____

_____

_____

The reports on "Returning Spirits"; "Spirits in Waiting"; "The Master Deceiver" and "The Thief Cometh" (These 'mystical' dreams and visions, their revelations and manifestations that took place):

_____

_____

_____

_____

What do you have to say overall about "Reflections of Spiritual Warnings?"

_____

_____

_____

_____

Do you believe these reports on Spiritual Warnings? _____ Yes_____ No

Do you share similar experiences of 'Spiritual Warnings' with the author?...

❖ **Has God ever 'divinely' intervened in any of your long-term relationships or friendships?**
_____ Yes_____ No

> ➤ DO NOT complete the [following] section if YOUR response was **'No'**

'Reflect' on (list) some of these personal, social, or business relationships of past you were involved in, that God delivered [saved] you from:

1 _____

2 _____

3 _____

4 _____

❖ **Has God ever warned you through a 'dream' or a 'vision'?** _____ Yes_____ No

> ➢ DO NOT complete this section if YOUR response was '**No**'

When you awoke from your <u>first</u> dream giving you a warning or, came to yourself after seeing your <u>first</u> vision of warning, were you aware it was from God? _____ Yes_____ No

When you awoke or came to yourself from your first dream or vision of warning, were you afraid and/or confused? _____ Yes_____ No

I have been warned of sins I have committed? _____ Yes_____ No

I have been warned of things that were hidden? _____ Yes_____ No

I have received warnings of the 'enemy's' presence in my life? _____ Yes_____ No

I have received warnings of the 'enemy's' presence in the life of someone I knew?
_____ Yes_____ No

If God <u>has</u> warned you of the 'enemy's presence concerning yourself or someone you knew, did you pray a 'prayer of protection' when you received warning? _____ Yes_____ No

Has any 'dreams or visions' of "Spiritual Warnings" come to pass? _____ Yes_____ No

If a 'dream or vision' of 'Spiritual Warning' <u>has</u> come to pass:

'Reflect' on one (1) of these dreams or visions: (Briefly describe the event that occurred whereby you knew in your spirit it was a 'divine' connection to the warning you received.)

_____

_____

_____

_____

Have you ever asked God to reveal things to you for protection, and when He did, you ignored His signs of warning? _____ Yes_____ No

Do you have "eyes to see?" _____ Yes _____ No _____ Not Sure

❖ **Have you been blessed with the gift of 'Spiritual discernment'?**
_____ Yes _____ No _____ Not Sure

Can you sense someone's 'negative' character? (Get an uneasy or eerie feeling inside around certain people or from a person when you first meet them) _____ Yes _____ No

Can you sense a 'negative' presence in an atmosphere? (Get an uneasy or eerie feeling inside when you enter into a room or in a certain environment) _____ Yes _____ No

[**Note:** If you sense things with a greater ability than normal intuition ('natural discernment'), more than likely, you have been blessed with the spiritual 'gift of discernment'].

❖ **Have you been blessed with the gift of 'Spiritual Warfare'?**
_____ Yes _____ No _____ Not Sure

Do you pray regularly for 'divine' protection over yourself, family and friends; for your home, church, work and finances? _____ Yes _____ No

Do you pray at times for 'divine' protection over your mind [thought patterns]; to remain sober; to refrain from worldly sin? _____ Yes _____ No

Do you feel the need at times (unction) to pray for other people [intercessory warfare] against the enemy and his 'negative' strongholds (spirits of vexation, infirmities, iniquities, etc.)?
_____ Yes _____ No

> ➢ DO NOT answer this *last* question if YOUR *last* response was **'No'**

Have you ever seen the face of a 'vexing (oppressing; tormenting) spirit' or a vision of infirmity (sickness or disease) while praying [having "eyes to see"]? _____ Yes _____ No

[**Note:** If you have seen <u>any</u> of these things while praying (interceding) for others, more than likely, you have been blessed with the 'gift of spiritual warfare' - a component of 'spiritual discernment'].

❖ **I *do not* have 'Reflections on Spiritual Warnings':** ☐

Do you believe that you are 'spirit'? _____ Yes _____ No

Do you believe God warns and protects His children? _____ Yes _____ No

Do you believe in 'Spiritual Attacks'? _____ Yes _____ No

Do you believe in the gift of 'Spiritual Warfare'? _____ Yes _____ No

❖ **What do you think about the [following] *'spiritual'* and *'mystical'* accounts?**

The report on "Vision of Spiritual Warfare" (Hearing the 'spiritual' voice, seeing the vision of warfare, and its revelation):

_____

_____

_____

_____

The report on "Dream of the Ring" (This 'mystical' dream, its revelations, interpretations and manifestation of 'deceitfulness' coming to pass):

_____

_____

_____

_____

The reports "Returning Spirits"; "Spirits in Waiting"; "The Master Deceiver"; and "The Thief Cometh" (These 'mystical' dreams and visions, their revelations and manifestations):

_____

_____

_____

_____

What do you have to say <u>overall</u> about "Reflections of Spiritual Warnings?"

_____

_____

_____

_____

Do you believe these reports of 'Spiritual Warnings'? _____ Yes _____ No

Testimonials

Have you ever been asked to go somewhere or be involved in something and a 'negative' feeling (bad vibe) came over you? _____ Yes_____ No

If you <u>have</u> sensed this feeling (whether you went or were involved), did you find out later that something 'negative' or 'bad' happened? _____ Yes_____ No

Have you ever planned to be somewhere on time, ending up running behind schedule, and on the road you were traveling or at the place of destination, a 'life-threatening' incident occurred just before your arrival? _____ Yes_____ No

If you have <u>had</u> this experience, did you consider the fact that if you were on schedule you could have been involved in the 'life-threatening' incident that occurred? _____ Yes_____ No

[**<u>Note:</u>** If you have had <u>any</u> of these experiences, know that it was God warning and protecting you. You never know 'who' or 'what' God may have been protecting (saving) you from.]

❖ **Has God ever 'divinely' intervened at the beginning of a relationship or friendship... giving you the first subtle, warning sign when:**

1. After being introduced to the person, you felt a bad vibe? _____ Yes_____ No

2. In public with this person for the first time, and they said something or did something, and you sensed in your heart [spirit] it was not the right thing to say or do? _____ Yes_____ No

❖ **Has God ever 'divinely' intervened in any of your long-term relationships or friendships?** _____ Yes_____ No_____ Not Sure

'Reflect' on (list) a couple of personal, social or business relationships of past that you were involved in - that ended - and you wondered (never knew) what happened to dissolve these relationships:

1_____

2_____

[**<u>Note:</u>** If you have had <u>any</u> of these experiences and ignored God's early warning signs to protect you, be watchful. This is how we wind up with someone 'out of the will of God' in our lives - that could eventually lead to a life in the 'Valley of Dry Bones'.]

If you have <u>had</u> any of these experiences and ignored them, did you learn from them? _____ Yes_____ No

Reflections of Spiritual Warnings:

If you completed "testimonials": You now have YOUR own 'Reflections' of "Immanuel" - God with us! (*Isaiah 7:13&14; Matthew 1:23*); revealing His absolute, supreme power as "Jehovah-Nissi" - the Lord that reigns in Victory! (*Exodus 17:15&16; Isaiah 12:2; 26:4*)

God's 'Warnings' conveyed through Dreams & Visions:

✓ Here are a few Scriptures revealing "warnings" from God conveyed through dreams and visions: Ezekiel; Daniel; and Matthew.

Chapter Reflections: (Write additional thoughts/feelings about this Chapter here:)

_____

_____

_____

_____

_____

_____

Chapter 9
Spiritual Attacks

Spiritual Attacks consists of encounters (accounts) of enemy efforts to try and hinder God's blessings upon your life (and your family's life) from coming into fruition (*manifesting*).

"For we wrestle not against flesh and blood, but against principalities, against powers, against the rulers of the darkness of this world, against spiritual wickedness in high places." - Ephesians 6:12.

"Be sober, be vigilant; because your adversary the devil, as a roaring lion, walketh about, seeking whom he may devour." - I Peter 5:8.

My Reflections:

I believe we wrestle against powers of 'spiritual' wickedness. _____ Yes _____ No

I believe in 'spiritual' attacks. _____ Yes _____ No

I have been "under enemy fire." _____ Yes _____ No

I have dreamed of being "under enemy fire." _____ Yes _____ No

I believe in the 'gift of spiritual warfare'. _____ Yes _____ No

I am a 'Spiritual Warrior'. _____ Yes _____ No

☐ I have 'Reflections of Spiritual Attacks'.
☐ I <u>do not</u> have 'Reflections on Spiritual Attacks'.

❖ **I have 'Reflections of Spiritual Attacks':** ☐

Testimonials

I have been manipulated by a person one time or another. (Unwillingly under their subtle influence or control; a 'negative' stronghold) _____ Yes _____ No

I have been victimized by a business or a person one time or another through a scheme of fraud or deceit. (Tricked [conned] to get my money, property, position, etc.) _____ Yes _____ No

There have been times in my life when it seemed as if the 'whole world' was against me at once for no reason at all (including family, friends, co-workers, etc). _____ Yes _____ No

'Reflect' on a couple of times when things were going great in your life and then, all of a sudden, it seemed as if anything 'negative' that could possibly happen, happened - concerning family, a relationship, home, work, church, finances, etc.:

1. _____

   _____

2. _____

   _____

❖ **What are your opinions of these *'spiritual'* and *'mystical'* enemy attacks?**

The reports "Under Enemy Fire" (The dream; revelations and manifestations):

_____

_____

_____

The report on "The Spirit of Death" [Chapter 2] (The letter, childhood experience and nightmares of death; their revelations and interpretations):

_____

_____

_____

_____

What do you have to say <u>overall</u> about "Reflections of Spiritual Attacks?"

_____

_____

_____

_____

Has the enemy ever tried killing you? _____ Yes_____ No

Has the enemy ever stolen from you; or destroyed things? _____ Yes_____ No

If the enemy <u>has stolen</u> or <u>destroyed things</u>, have you taken back what was stolen, or rebuilt what was destroyed? _____ Yes_____ No

Do you share similar experiences of *'Spiritual Attacks'* with the author?...

❖ **I have experienced a *'negative'* force in my life.** _____ Yes_____ No

> ➤ DO NOT complete this section if YOUR response was **'No'**

> ➤ Respond to (1) of the (2) sections that apply to you.

☐ **I am *no longer* under 'spiritual' attack:**

Did this 'negative' force affect your daily living? _____ Yes _____ No

Did you experience 'tormenting' nightmares? (Causing you to awake from your sleep in fear of someone or something) _____ Yes _____ No

Were you able to identify the 'negative' force(s)? _____ Yes _____ No

Were you able to identify its source(s) [root cause]? _____ Yes _____ No

During these attacks, had God recently promised you something? Were 'blessings or a miracle' from God beginning to manifest in your life? _____ Yes _____ No

Do you believe it was God who 'divinely' intervened? (Delivered you from the 'snare' [trap] of the enemy) _____ Yes _____ No

How did God deliver you from this 'negative' force? (Describe your deliverance):

_____

_____

_____

_____

_____

_____

☐ **I am _presently_ under 'spiritual' attack:**

Is this 'negative' force affecting any of your daily living routines? _____ Yes _____ No

Is this 'negative' force affecting your health? _____ Yes _____ No

If affecting your daily living routines or your health, describe how this force is interfering:

_____

_____

_____

_____

_____

_____

Are you able to identify the 'negative' force(s)? _____ Yes _____ No

Are you able to identify its source(s) [root cause]? _____ Yes _____ No

Has God recently promised you something? (Are you expecting 'blessings or a miracle from God' to manifest in your life?) _____ Yes _____ No

Is this 'negative' force stemming from someone in your life who is 'out of the will of God' (a hindrance to you)? _____ Yes _____ No

Are you experiencing 'tormenting' nightmares? (Causing you to awake from your sleep at night in fear of someone or something) _____ Yes _____ No

Have you prayed for deliverance from this 'predicament'? _____ Yes _____ No

[**Note:** If you have never prayed for deliverance, now is the time to start! Continue to spend 'time with God.' Meditate on _Psalms 23; 91; 119_ and _Ephesians 1:17-21._]

❖ **Have you learned the 'Art of Spiritual Warfare'?** _____ Yes _____ No

> ➤ DO NOT complete this section if YOUR response was '**No**'

I suit up daily with the armour of God. (_Ephesians 6:13-18_) _____ Yes _____ No

I pray daily over my life (mind, health, family, friends, home, church, work, finances) and against wiles [tricks] of the enemy. _____ Yes_____ No

I come out of battles 'victoriously' (carrying "victories of the cross" along with faith in the "blood of Jesus" - these are my weapons of 'spiritual' warfare). _____ Yes_____ No

Briefly describe changes that have taken place in your way of thinking (belief; thought patterns) since coming into revelation of 'spiritual' wickedness:

_____

_____

_____

_____

❖ **I _do not_ have 'Reflections on Spiritual Attacks':** ☐

❖ **What are your opinions of these *'spiritual'* and *'mystical'* enemy attacks?**

The reports "Under Enemy Fire" (The dream; revelations and manifestations):

_____

_____

_____

_____

The report on "The Spirit of Death" [Chapter 2] (The letter, childhood experience and nightmares of death; their revelations and interpretations):

_____

_____

_____

_____

What do you have to say <u>overall</u> about "Reflections of Spiritual Attacks?"

_____

_____

_____

_____

Has the enemy ever tried to kill you? _____ Yes _____ No

Has the enemy ever stolen from you and/or destroyed things? _____ Yes _____ No

If the enemy has stolen or destroyed things, have you taken back what was stolen, or rebuilt what was destroyed? _____ Yes _____ No

Testimonials

Have you ever been manipulated by a person one time or another? (Unknowingly under their subtle influence or control; a 'negative' stronghold) _____ Yes _____ No

Have you ever been victimized by a business or a person through a scheme of fraud or deceit? (Tricked [conned] to get your money, property, position, etc.) _____ Yes _____ No

Have you ever been in certain predicaments and/or circumstances and wondered "How you wind up in such a mess?" _____ Yes _____ No

Have you ever experienced 'tormenting' nightmares? (Causing you to awake from your sleep in fear of someone or something) _____ Yes _____ No

Have you ever considered the "cause" and "affect" of these instances? _____ Yes _____ No

Do you believe in 'spiritual' wickedness? _____ Yes _____ No

If you believe in 'spiritual' wickedness, briefly describe changes that have taken place in your way of thinking (belief; thought patterns) since coming into revelation of 'spiritual' wickedness:

_____

_____

_____

_____

Have there ever been times in your life when it seemed as if the 'whole world' was against you at once, for no reason at all (including family, friends, co-workers, etc.)? _____ Yes _____ No

'Reflect' on a couple of times when things were going great in your life and then, all of a sudden, it seemed as if anything 'negative' that could possibly happen, happened - concerning family, a relationship, home, church, work, finances, etc.:

1. _____

_____

2. _____

_____

[**_Note:_** All of these experiences could have well been 'Spiritual Attacks'. The enemy comes to steal, kill, and destroy. He will use anybody or anything to disrupt your life, to steal your peace of mind.]

"Be sober, be vigilant; because your adversary the devil, as a roaring lion, walketh about, seeking whom he may devour." - I Peter 5:8

- Although your adversary the devil, as a roaring lion, walketh about, seeking whom he may devour, <u>do not</u> let his 'roar' (loud noise - attack) frighten you, there is no way that he can devour you (take complete control over your life). The 'blood of Jesus' will never lose its power!

- When you are under God's 'divine' protection - abiding under the shadow of the Almighty - He will fight your battles (protect you) even if you are not a 'Spiritual Warrior'; if God is for you, then who can stand against you? (*Joshua 1:5*).

Reflections of Spiritual Attacks:

> If you completed "testimonials": You now have [more] 'Reflections' of "Jehovah-Nissi" - the "Lord that reigns in Victory." *(Exodus 17:15&16)*.

✓ Know (understand) that the Kingdom of God is at war with the enemy - even though the battle has already been won in the spirit realm. Death has been defeated; Jesus has the keys to life and death (*Revelation 1:18*).

However, as children of God, we are constantly under enemy fire (attack). The enemy is warring against us because we are part of God's victorious army; soldiers willing to "fight the good fight of faith" while living in the earthly realm (*I Timothy 6:12*).

✓ We fight 'spiritual battles' every day in our home, church, family, workplace, finances, etc. When certain daily 'negative' circumstances or situations arise, we are facing 'spiritual warfare'. This is why we must suit up daily with the whole armour of God. (*Ephesians 6:11*).

✓ Remember, we are presently living in the natural world. Therefore, even though these attacks are spiritual, they will manifest in the natural. So, if you have not suited up, suit up! And if you have already suited up - "Stand at Attention" and "Keep Watching!"

Chapter Reflections: (Write additional thoughts/feelings about this Chapter here:)

_____

_____

_____

_____

_____

_____

Chapter 10

Spiritual Deliverance

When the time is right, a child of God will receive affirmations from God (through revelations from prophecy received, answered prayer requests, and dreams dreamed and visions seen) confirming His release of them to step out to be who it is that He has called them to be.

We can be delivered from many things; set free over and over again. But 'true' spiritual deliverance breaks all strongholds [brings Salvation] and instills within a balance of 'spiritual' harmony (peace within; peace is a gift from God).

My Reflections:

I have come to know 'Truth'; I was once blind, but now I see. _____ Yes _____ No

I have been redeemed (restored; resurrected) from a life of bondage (slavery; sin). _____ Yes _____ No

I have been transformed into a 'new creation in Christ'. _____ Yes _____ No

I believe in the promises and blessings of God (including miracles). _____ Yes _____ No

I have come into 'the will of God' for my life. _____ Yes _____ No

I have embraced the new me; I am 'fearfully and wonderfully' made. _____ Yes _____ No

☐ I have 'Reflections of Spiritual Deliverance'.

☐ I do not have 'Reflections on Spiritual Deliverance'.

> ➢ Complete (1) of (2) Main Sections based on YOUR response to "Spiritual Deliverance"

❖ **I have 'Reflections of Spiritual Deliverance':** ☐

"I sought the Lord, and he answered me; he delivered me from all of my fears." - Psalm 34:4

Testimonials

God's 'amazing grace' has delivered me and set me free. _____ Yes_____ No

I believe "all things work together for good to them that love God, to them who are the called according to his purpose" (*Romans 8:28*). _____ Yes _____ No

I have gifts of "wisdom, knowledge and understanding." _____ Yes_____ No

I am living a "blessed" life. (A 'prosperous' and 'peaceful' life) _____ Yes_____ No

I am proclaiming 'true' Salvation. (Total deliverance; works and gifts of the 'Holy Spirit' are visible in my life) _____ Yes_____ No

I am 'fearfully' and 'wonderfully' made. _____ Yes_____ No

I am a 'vessel of honour' (useful for the 'Master's' good works). _____ Yes_____ No

After coming into revelation God had actually delivered you and set you free (redeemed and transformed you), did your desire to live by God's will become great? _____ Yes _____ No

After being 'born again' (accepting Jesus Christ as Lord and Saviour, receiving Salvation, and renewing your mind), did it matter what family and friends perceived of you?
_____ Yes_____ No

Did family and friends find it hard to believe how the Lord was working in (blessing) YOUR life?
_____ Yes_____ No

Do you find YOUR 'Reflections of Spiritual Deliverance' hard to believe at times?
_____ Yes _____ No

(If not already), would you be willing to share your 'Reflections of Spiritual Deliverance' with someone else 'presently' experiencing predicaments and/or circumstances of your past?
_____ Yes_____ No

❖ **What are your opinions of these "life-changing"** *'spiritual'* **accounts:**

The report on "Vision of Destiny" ("Purpose & Destiny" ["the Lord's work"] unveiled; the vision and its revelations):

_____

_____

_____

_____

The report on "Promises from God" (Revelation promising "something really special" in the life of the author):

_____

_____

_____

_____

The reports on "Acceptance of God's Calling" (These accounts and their revelations) :

_____

_____

_____

_____

The reports on "New Birth" (These 'mystical' dreams on 'spiritual birth'; their revelations and prophetic interpretations):

_____

_____

_____

_____

What do you have to say <u>overall</u> about "Reflections of Spiritual Deliverance?"

_____

_____

_____

_____

Do you believe these reports of 'Spiritual Deliverance'? _____ Yes_____ No

Do you share similar experiences of *'Spiritual Deliverance'* with the author?...

❖ **Has God ever *'personally'* promised YOU anything?...**

Although God has made many 'corporate' [mutual] promises to man, has He 'personally' spoken to you (your spirit), or birthed something inside of you revealing His will [desires] for you through a prophecy, dream or vision? _____ Yes _____ No

Have you been 'spiritually' promoted (to perform Kingdom work) whereby 'treasures' are being stored in heaven? _____ Yes _____ No

Have you ever witnessed a miracle? (A manifestation [sign or demonstration] that only God had power to do) _____ Yes _____ No

> ➤ DO NOT complete this section if YOUR *last* response was **'No'**

What did God miraculously do? (Briefly describe this supernatural account):

_____

_____

_____

_____

Was it YOUR miracle that you witnessed? _____ Yes _____ No

❖ **Are you presently 'expecting' a miracle?** (A manifestation [demonstration] of the 'impossible' in your life) _____ Yes _____ No

> ➤ DO NOT complete this section if YOUR response was **'No'**

What are you expecting that would seem 'impossible' to the people who know you? (Describe this expected 'perfect' and 'complete' work):

_____

_____

_____

_____

When this miracle <u>comes to pass</u> (manifest in the natural what was conceived in your spirit), would you consider it a 'Spiritual Conception'? _____ Yes _____ No

❖ **Has God called you to work directly in (or with an organization for) the Church?**
_____ Yes _____ No _____ Not Sure

"And God hath set some in the church, first apostles, secondarily prophets, thirdly teachers, after that miracles, then gifts of healing, helps, governments, diversities of tongues." - I Corinthians 12:28.

Do you enjoy helping others? (Volunteering your services; blessing others - family, friends, neighbors or people you do not know - by doing things for them or giving to them unexpectedly) _____ Yes_____ No

Do you have any Spiritual gifts (blessings; an anointing) or natural talents (skills), that you are aware of, useful for the uplifting of the 'Body of Christ'? _____ Yes_____ No

'Reflect' on (list) a couple of times when 'spiritually' lead to perform certain tasks (usually performed by people working in or for the Church) you would have never ordinarily done, or thought of doing, on your own cognizance. (Briefly describe service or work done):

1_____

2_____

Is there a 'special' call on your life? (An anointing for a special 'appointment' or 'service' inside of or directly for the Church) _____ Yes_____ No

> DO NOT complete this section if YOUR response was 'No'

If God has called you to Work (Service) directly inside [or for] the Church:

Have you accepted your 'special' call? (No longer in denial) _____ Yes_____ No

Are you (or were you) fearful of your 'special' call? (Fearful of giving your will to accept God's will; or how other people will (would) perceive you) _____ Yes_____ No

What work has God called you to do? (Describe appointed [chosen] position whereby using your special 'gifts and talents' - e.g., leadership work, servant ship, administrative work, teaching, missionary work, etc.):

_____

_____

_____

_____

Are you 'presently' walking in your 'special' calling? (Performing works [services] God has called you to) _____ Yes_____ No

[*"...To whom men have committed much, of him they will ask the more."* - Luke 12:48. There is much responsibility when it comes to performing work (service) within or directly for the Church.]

"The secret of the Lord is with them that fear Him; and He will show them his covenant." - Psalm 25:14.

Are you proclaiming 'true' Salvation? (Total deliverance; whereby works of the Lord and gifts of the Spirit are visible in your life) _____ Yes_____ No

❖ **What are opinions of these "life-changing" _'spiritual'_ accounts:**

The report on "Vision of Destiny" ("Purpose & Destiny" ["the Lord's work"] unveiled; the vision and its revelation):

_____

_____

_____

_____

The report on "Promises from God" (Revelation promising "something really special" in the life of the author):

_____

_____

_____

_____

The reports on "Acceptance of God's Calling" (These accounts and their revelations):

_____

_____

_____

_____

The reports on "New Birth" (These 'mystical' dreams on 'spiritual birth'; their revelations and prophetic interpretations):

_____

_____

_____

_____

What do you have to say <u>overall</u> about "Reflections of Spiritual Deliverance?"

_____

_____

_____

_____

Do you believe the reports on 'Reflections of Spiritual Deliverance'? _____ Yes_____ No

❖ **After accepting Jesus Christ as your Savior, did you go through any type (form) of 'Spiritual Deliverance'?** _____ Yes_____ No

| Respond to (1) of the (2) sections that apply to you: |

☐ **I have been through 'spiritual' deliverance:**

| **_Testimonials_** |

Did you truly repent? (Old things have passed away; you have totally given up the will of your flesh - _Psalm 94:9-11_) _____ Yes_____ No

Are you presently living a 'prosperous' and 'peaceful' life? _____ Yes_____ No

Do you believe "all things work together for good to them that love God, to them who are the called according to His purpose" (_Romans 8:28_)? _____ Yes _____ No

Have you seen God's 'Master' plan for your life? _____ Yes_____ No

If you <u>have</u> been through spiritual deliverance [after receiving Salvation], why is it that you <u>do not</u> have 'Reflections of Spiritual Deliverance'? (Explain YOUR predicament):

_____

_____

_____

Were you totally delivered (from sinful iniquities, worldly traditions, demonic strongholds)?

1) Are there any emotional scars (bitterness, unforgiveness, rejection, etc.) from others that remain rooted within you, that need to be released? _____ Yes_____ No

2) Are there any secret (hidden, grievous and/or oppressing) sins that you must confess, repent of, and forgive yourself of? [Study _Psalm 94:9-11_.] _____ Yes_____ No

3) Do you believe that you are a 'vessel of honour' (sanctified, useful to the 'Master', and prepared unto every good work)? _____ Yes_____ No

☐ **I have *never* been through 'spiritual' deliverance:**

Did you repent of your sins upon receiving Salvation? _____ Yes_____ No

Have you changed your way of thinking (from the way the world thinks to 'Godly' thinking)? ["Renewed your mind" - *Romans 12:2, 21*] _____ Yes_____ No

Would you be 'willing' to receive deliverance (let go of everything) to become a 'vessel of honor' (useful for the Master's good works) - living by the 'law of the Spirit'? _____ Yes_____ No

If 'willing' to receive deliverance:

1) Are you aware that 'repentance' means to <u>never</u> do the same sinful thing again (and not just an 'emotion' being sorrowful for sinful things that you do - then, turn around and do these same sinful things over and over again)? _____ Yes_____ No

2) Are there any secret (hidden, grievous and/or oppressing) sins that must be confessed, repented of, and that you must forgive yourself of? [Study *Psalm 94:9-11.*]
   a. _____ Yes_____ No

3) Are there any emotional scars (bitterness, unforgiveness, rejection, etc.) from others rooted within you, which need to be released? _____ Yes_____ No

Reflections of Spiritual Deliverance:

> If you completed "testimonials": You now have more 'Reflections' of "Jehovah-Nissi" - the "Lord that reigns in Victory." *(Exodus 17:15&16).*

✓ Spiritual deliverance (living by the 'law of the Spirit') is part of the 'Salvation' process.

✓ Spiritual deliverance is what one must go through in order to receive "total" deliverance [true Salvation]? [Study *I & II Peter*]. (This includes deliverance from sinful iniquities [self] and various other 'negative' spiritual strongholds of vexations, addictions and afflictions.)

"Lay not up for yourselves treasures upon earth, where moth and rust doth corrupt, and where thieves break through and steal: But lay up for yourselves treasures in heaven, where neither moth nor rust doth corrupt, and where thieves do not break through nor steal: For where your treasure is, there will your heart be also." - Matthew 6:19-21.

Chapter Reflections: (Write additional thoughts/feelings about this Chapter here:)

_____

_____

_____

_____

_____

_____

Chapter 11

Exiting the Valley

BRANCH OF THE VINE

"I am the true vine, and my Father is the husbandman. Every branch in me that beareth not fruit he taketh away: and every branch that beareth fruit, he purgeth (prunes) it, that it may bring forth more fruit. Now you are clean (pruned) through the word which I have spoken unto you" - John 15:1-3.

"I am the vine, you are the branches: He that abideth in me, and I in him, the same bringeth forth much fruit; for without (apart from) me ye can do nothing. If a man abide not in me, he is cast forth as a branch, and is withered; and men gather them, and cast them into the fire, and they are burned." - John 15:5 & 6.

My Reflections:

I know what it feels like to be cast forth as a branch; and withered. _____ Yes _____ No

I have been 'tried and tested' by God. _____ Yes _____ No

I have received many 'spiritual' breakthroughs. _____ Yes _____ No

I have learned what it means to sow seed 'among good ground'. _____ Yes _____ No

I am no longer in the 'wilderness' (The Valley). _____ Yes _____ No

☐ I have 'Reflections of Exiting the Valley'.

☐ I <u>do not</u> have 'Reflections on Exiting the Valley'.

> ➤ Complete (1) of (2) Main Sections based on YOUR response to "Exiting the Valley."

❖ **I have 'Reflections of Exiting the Valley':** ☐

"And he shall be like a tree that's planted by the rivers water, that bringeth forth his fruit in season; his leaf also shall not wither; and whatsoever he doeth shall prosper." - Psalm 1:3

> ➤ Check the (1) box that 'presently' describes your life predicament:

- I <u>am</u> "Exiting the Valley" - at the crossing of the 'River Jordan'. ☐

- I <u>have</u> "Exited the Valley" - on my way into the 'Promised Land'. ☐

- I have "Entered the Promised Land" - God's Promises are being released unto me. ☐

Testimonials

God (the 'heavenly' Father) is the 'head' of my life. _____ Yes _____ No

I have discovered many of God's heavenly treasures. _____ Yes _____ No

I have received many 'spiritual' breakthroughs. _____ Yes _____ No

I have come into revelation [knowledge] of my 'true' Purpose & Destiny. _____ Yes _____ No

I have a planting from the Lord (no more voids within; only the 'joy of the Lord' remains). _____ Yes_____ No

I am cultivating seeds sown (remaining faithful in my works; bearing fruit that is productive). _____ Yes _____ No

The 'spiritual' meaning of the 'Number 7' is defined as "Perfection" or "Completion." Can you list (7) blessings of 'Thanksgiving': (Works God has <u>perfected</u> in your life; things or predicaments God has <u>completely</u> delivered you from - things that are over!)

1_____

2_____

3_____

4_____

5_____

6_____

7_____

God has released (releasing) 'the impossible' in my life? _____ Yes _____ No

Do you share similar experiences of *'Exiting the Valley'* with the author?...

❖ **Have you reached heights ("Mountain Highs") you never dreamed of reaching?**
_____ Yes _____ No

> ➢ DO NOT complete this section if YOUR response was **'No'**

Does 'new heights' include provisions from 'dreams dreamed' and/or 'visions seen'?
_____ Yes _____ No

Does 'new heights' include works that are satisfying to God (whereby 'treasures' are being stored in heaven)? _____ Yes _____ No

In attempting to reach 'new heights', did you become 'relentless'? (Unyielding, remaining steadfast in faith) _____ Yes _____ No

In attempting to reach 'new heights', did you take certain things by force? (Not by your might, but by the power of the 'Spirit of the Living God' that is) _____ Yes _____ No

Have you come into both the 'mutual' promises of God and things He has 'personally' promised you? (Deuteronomy 28:1-14) _____ Yes _____ No

I have come into things that seemed 'impossible'! _____ Yes _____ No

❖ **Are you "walking with God?"...**

Trusting and believing in Him, His word and His will [love] for you; staying on the path of righteousness. _____ Yes _____ No

> ➢ DO NOT complete this section if YOUR response was **'No'**

I eat of His daily bread. (Live by the 'Living word' of God) _____ Yes_____ No

I am a receiver of His daily blessings. (I have 'spiritual' wealth) _____ Yes_____ No

I am walking upright; remaining steadfast, faithful and obedient. _____ Yes _____ No

I have taken 'dominion' over my life (with a new outlook, walking in 'power' and 'authority').
_____ Yes_____ No

I have passed the interview that one must pass (final test [trial] involving challenges of faith) to attain a position of "power and authority" in the Kingdom of God (*Job 23:10-17; Psalm 17:3; I Peter 1:6&7; 4:12&13*). _____ Yes _____ No

I am 'fearfully' and 'wonderfully' made. _____ Yes_____ No

I have 'Assurance of Salvation' (*II Timothy 3:14-17*). _____ Yes _____ No

❖ **Has God given you *any* 'new' directions lately?** _____ Yes _____ No

*If God **has** given you 'new' direction:*

Would you consider this new direction (or assignment) one of great 'honor' and 'privilege'? _____ Yes _____ No

In what direction you are headed? or, What is your new assignment? (Describe God's will for you at this time, or your new position for performing Kingdom work):

Direction: _____

_____

_____

Instructions:_____

_____

_____

_____

_____

Have you ever started a God-given "work" [task] and then, did not finish [complete] it? _____ Yes _____ No

❖ **I *do not* have 'Reflections on Exiting the Valley':** ☐

"Hope (dreams) deferred maketh the heart sick; but when the desire cometh, it is a tree of life." - Proverb 13:12.

> ➤ Check the (1) box that 'presently' describes your life predicament:

- ▪ I <u>never</u> left "Egypt" - I'm still in bondage; accepting life as it is. ☐

- ▪ I <u>am still</u> "In the Valley" - Wandering in the wilderness; in need of direction. ☐

- ▪ I am "Exiting the Valley" - Crossing the River Jordan; walking in a new direction. ☐

Are you wrestling with God (sowing seeds in many wrong places)? _____ Yes_____ No

Do you still have pain imparted by others rooted within? _____ Yes _____ No

Do you feel like a 'withered' branch (living apart from the Father)? _____ Yes _____ No

Are you living life far below your own expectations - let alone the expectations of God? _____ Yes _____ No

Are you looking forward to being released to go forth into that which God has called you to? _____ Yes _____ No

Wouldn't you like to know how it feels to be 'like a tree planted by the rivers water'?
...the Spirit of the Living God flowing through you, having all of your hearts desires:

Testimonials

The 'spiritual' meaning of the 'Number 7' is defined as "Perfection" or "Completion." Can you list (7) blessings of 'Thanksgiving'? (Works God has perfected in your life; predicaments or things God has completely delivered you from - that are over!):

1 _____
2 _____
3 _____
4 _____
5 _____
6 _____
7 _____

Envision (imagine; see) yourself right now, at this very moment, having the 'Spirit of the Living God' flowing through you, and all that your heart's desires. NOW... briefly describe how this 'glorious' vision just seen made you feel inside:

_____

_____

_____

_____

Would you be willing to do what one must do to gain access to these 'wonderful, glorious' desires you just envisioned for your life? _____ Yes _____ No

❖ **Are you willing to make God 'head' of your life?...**

Have you acquainted [reacquainted] yourself with His ways? _____ Yes _____ No

Do you understand what it means to "walk with God"? _____ Yes _____ No

Has God been "trying you" and "testing you?" (For you to know Him and to love Him)
_____ Yes _____ No _____ Not Sure

Have you been faced with various "measures of fire?" (Tests [trials] involving 'challenges of faith')
_____ Yes _____ No

When faced with <u>certain</u> predicaments or circumstances, do you ever ask yourself, "What would be the right (Godly) thing to do?" before responding or reacting. _____ Yes _____ No

After 'Exiting the Valley", would you be willing to "walk by faith and not by sight?" (Keeping your eyes on the "bigness of God" and not on the "vanities of this world".) _____ Yes _____ No

If God <u>has</u> "tried and tested" you:

Have you passed many tests? (Come out of predicaments and/or circumstances with 'positive' expectations, results or actions) _____ Yes _____ No

Have you ever started a God-given "work" ["task"] and then, did not finish [complete] it?
_____ Yes _____ No

What was the last test (challenge of faith) that you passed? (Briefly describe this test [trial] and how you handled it):

_____

_____

_____

_____

During these tests ("measures of fire and faith"), did you cry 'tears of joy' and 'tears of pain'?
_____ Yes _____ No

Are you closer to your dreams? (Being who it is God has called you to be) _____ Yes _____ No

Has God given you any 'new' tests lately? _____ Yes _____ No

If God <u>has</u> given you a 'new' test:

Briefly describe this 'new' test <u>and</u> what it is that you must do in order to pass it. (Fulfill this assignment "to come forth as gold" - *Job 23:10*):

Test: _____

_____

_____

Instructions: _____

_____

_____

_____

_____

Has this test [trial] been 'trying' (challenging and demanding)? _____ Yes _____ No

Do you feel that you are 'equipped' (with God-given ability) to pass this new test, to go on to fulfill other assignments? (*Job 23:11& 12*) _____ Yes _____ No

Reflections of Exiting the Valley:

> If you completed "testimonials": You now have YOUR own 'Reflections' of "the True Vine" - *(John 15:1-5)* purging and cleansing you - preparing you to be "a vessel unto honor, useful for the 'Master's' good works."

✓ We all experience peaks of "Valley Los" at times in life. What's important is how we handle these situations while in them. Many 'valley experiences' are to draw us closer to God. Each time we come out, we should be walking further (on the path) towards the direction "God wills for our life."

✓ We have been set free through bloodshed by Jesus Christ upon the cross, and no longer have to go throughout life stuck in the wilderness - continuously living like "love don't love nobody."

✓ There has never been a time when God has appointed an assignment or promised something and <u>not</u> give His 'divine' instruction (God-given ability; guidance) on how to accomplish the assignment or to fulfill His promise.

✓ Follow God's directions and continue in His statutes - doing what He expects of you. During these 'trying' tests ("measures of fire and faith") remember that God loves you, will never leave you nor forsake you. *(Job; I Peter 1:6 & 7, 4:12 & 13).*

✓ Children of God who remain 'steadfast in faith' walk with God. Trusting in Him, remaining obedient, being bold and persistent; reaching "deep" levels of faith, thereby growing greater in grace.

Chapter Reflections: (Write additional thoughts/feelings about this Chapter here):

_____

_____

_____

_____

_____

_____

Chapter 12

Prophecies Fulfilled

$\mathcal{I}$f you have ever been given 'true' prophecy, whatever it is that God has promised you, certain of these promises may have already manifested (or began to manifest) in your life and you did not have "eyes to see."

My Reflections:

"You're Worthy!"

Has anyone ever promised you a gift, and after coming into revelation of the "bigness" of the gift, you felt that you were unworthy (undeserving of such a gift)? _____ Yes _____ No

I have been blessed with 'Spiritual' blessings. _____ Yes _____ No

I believe in the Spiritual 'gift of Prophecy'. _____ Yes _____ No

I have been given Prophecy. _____ Yes _____ No

I have received 'true' Prophecy. _____ Yes _____ No

I have Prophecy that has been fulfilled. _____ Yes _____ No

☐ I have 'Reflections of Prophecy Fulfilled'.

☐ I <u>do not</u> have 'Reflections on Prophecy Fulfilled'.

☐ I <u>do not</u> believe in Prophecy.

❖ **I have 'Reflections of Prophecy Fulfilled':** ☐

Testimonials

I have received 'true' Prophecy (a message from God) that has manifested in my life.
_____ Yes _____ No

Have you been given many prophecies? _____ Yes_____ No

If you <u>have</u> been given many prophecies, 'Reflect' on (list) at least (3) of these Prophecies:

1_____

2_____

3_____

Did you <u>receive</u> (believe; have faith in) these prophecies when given to you? _____ Yes _____ No

Did any of these prophecies reveal Spiritual 'gifts and talents'? _____ Yes_____ No

If prophecy <u>revealed</u> 'Spiritual' gifts, which gifts have you been blessed to receive? [Do not include the 'gift of Salvation' or the 'gift of the Holy Spirit'].

_____   _____

_____   _____

_____   _____

If prophecy <u>revealed</u> 'natural' talent(s), what talent(s) has God equipped you with? (Describe what you enjoy doing most - What you are passionate about? What skill do you do best?):

_____

_____

_____

Are you 'operating' in (or developing) your 'gifts and talents'? _____ Yes_____ No

If '<u>operating</u>' in your 'gifts and talents' are you using them to perform <u>any</u> Kingdom work? (Romans 12:4-8) _____ Yes_____ No

[**_Note:_** All 'Kingdom work' does not consist of work within the Church [building]. Work may consist of developing and using your gifts and talents to help people inside or outside of the Church].

Did any prophecy 'reveal' your Purpose and/or Destiny? _____ Yes _____ No

Did you feel 'worthy' of what was revealed unto you? (Being who God has planned for you to be and the life He has prepared for you in this earthly realm)_____ Yes_____ No

What do you have to say <u>overall</u> about "Reflections on Prophecies Fulfilled?":

_____

_____

_____

_____

Did any of these reports on 'Reflections of Prophecies Fulfilled' confirm [solidify] for you that 'true' prophecy speaks for itself? _____ Yes _____ No

Do you share similar experiences of *"Prophecy Fulfilled"* with the author?
_____ Yes _____ No

> ➢ DO NOT complete this section if YOUR response was **'No'**

Briefly describe one (1) "extra special" prophecy that has been fulfilled: (Things that took place regarding its manifestation.)

_____

_____

_____

_____

_____

_____

What 'special conditions' did you meet to help bring this "extra special" prophecy to pass? (Describe 'sacrifices' you made):

_____

_____

_____

_____

_____

Did you keep watch over this prophecy? (Events that occurred, to see if they lined up with what was prophesied to you?) _____ Yes _____ No

Was "Prophecy Fulfilled" worth the sacrifices you made? _____ Yes _____ No

Did you leave anyone or anything behind? _____ Yes _____ No

Was the "Prophecy Fulfilled" worth the wait? _____ Yes _____ No

Did you wait long for this prophecy to come to pass (manifest)? _____ Yes _____ No

When YOUR prophecy came to pass, were you surprised at its manifestation?
_____ Yes _____ No

Did you share YOUR prophecy with anyone? _____ Yes _____ No

If you shared YOUR prophecy: When it came to pass was the person (or people) with whom you shared YOUR prophecy surprised at its manifestation? (The "works of the Lord" in your life")
_____ Yes _____ No

Are you waiting for other prophecies to manifest? _____ Yes _____ No

[*"For unto whomsoever much is given, of him shall be much required..."* (Luke 12:48). There is much responsibility to fulfill on the receivers end in order for an "extra special" prophecy (God's 'perfect' plans) to manifest in one's life].

❖ **I *do not* have 'Reflections on Prophecy Fulfilled':** ☐

What do you have to say overall about "Reflections Prophecies Fulfilled?" (Express your feelings about the 'spiritual' gifts and 'natural' talents revealed through prophecies received; the revelations and manifestations of these accounts):

_____

_____

_____

_____

Did any of these reports on "Prophecies Fulfilled" confirm [solidify] for you that 'true' prophecy speaks for itself? _____ Yes _____ No

❖ **Have you ever been given a Prophecy?** _____ Yes _____ No _____ Not Sure

Has anyone ever come up to you - especially someone you did not know - while at Church, the mall, your work place, on the street, etc., and began speaking things to you concerning:

- Your life's "predicament or circumstance"? _____ Yes _____ No
- Your "gifts" and "talents"? _____ Yes _____ No
- Your "heart's desires"? _____ Yes _____ No
- Things about your future? _____ Yes _____ No

[**Note:** If you answered "**Yes**" to <u>any</u> question, more than likely, you have been given a prophecy. And if <u>any</u> of these things were present or have come to pass in your life, more than likely, you were given 'true' Prophecy.]

> Respond to (1) of the (2) sections that apply to you:

☐ **I _have_ been given a Prophecy:**

Testimonials

Did you <u>receive</u> (believe; have faith in) your prophecy (prophecies)? _____ Yes _____ No

Have you been given many prophecies? _____ Yes _____ No

If you <u>have</u> been given many prophecies, 'Reflect' on (list) at least (2) of these Prophecies:

1 _____

2 _____

Did prophecy reveal Spiritual 'gifts' and/or 'talents'? _____ Yes _____ No

If a prophecy <u>revealed</u> 'Spiritual' gifts, which gifts have you been blessed to receive? [Do not include the 'gift of Salvation' or the 'gift of the Holy Spirit'.]

    _____   _____

    _____   _____

    _____   _____

If a prophecy <u>revealed</u> 'natural' talent(s), what talent(s) has God equipped you with? (Describe the type of work you do, or skill(s) that you enjoy doing most - What you are passionate about? What do you do best?):

_____

_____

_____

Are you 'operating' in (or developing) your 'gifts and talents'? _____ Yes _____ No

If 'operating' in your 'gifts and talents,' are you using them to perform any Kingdom work/ service? (Romans 12:4-8) _____ Yes _____ No

Did any of these prophecies reveal your Purpose and/or Destiny? _____ Yes _____ No

Did you feel 'worthy' of what was revealed unto you? (Becoming who God has planned for you to be and the life He has prepared for you) _____ Yes _____ No

What did your last prophecy reveal? (Briefly summarize the message delivered):

_____

_____

_____

If you <u>believe</u> you have received 'true' Prophecy:

Did you make /or are you making the sacrifices necessary [meet the 'special conditions'] to help bring the prophecy to pass? _____ Yes _____ No

Did you at least wait on it to see if it would come to pass (manifest)? _____ Yes _____ No

If <u>presently</u> waiting on a Prophecy to manifest:

Are you waiting on God (the gatekeeper) for His 'divine' guidance? _____ Yes _____ No

Are you watching over this prophecy? (Watching events that occur in YOUR life, to see if they line up with what was prophesized to you?) _____ Yes _____ No

Have you waited long for this prophecy to come to pass? _____ Yes _____ No

How long are you willing to wait? ..."*It is not for you to know the times or the seasons, which the Father hath put in his own power.*" - Acts 1:7

[*Note:* If you <u>have met</u> the 'special conditions' of your prophecy, but you are <u>not</u> watching over it: How do you know that YOUR prophecy did not come to pass or, begin to manifest in your life? (An event may have already occurred, or work that you have already done, could have led to this prophecy coming to pass!)]

☐   **I have <u>*never*</u> been given a Prophecy:**

Testimonials

If 'true' Prophecy was delivered to you in your future, would you be willing to wait on God (the gatekeeper) for His 'divine' guidance? _____ Yes _____ No

If <u>willing</u> to wait on God:

How long would you be willing to wait? _____

And if YOUR Prophecy came to pass, would you share this "mystery" (hidden truth) with someone else? (Minister to others to help them understand and believe in this invaluable 'gift of Prophecy')
_____ Yes _____ No

[***<u>Note</u>:*** When given your first prophecy, you will <u>know</u> whether it is a 'true' prophecy; you will "receive it" in your spirit - have faith in it and believe it. *"The Spirit itself beareth witness with our spirit"* (Romans 8:16)].

❖ **I *<u>do not</u>* believe in Prophecy:** ☐

[NOTE: Take a moment before responding to these Reflections. In an instant, you will be amazed at what will be revealed. Things you never took time to understand, now is the time to "Learn what it all means!"]

Have you been blessed with 'natural' talents? _____ Yes _____ No

If blessed <u>with</u> 'natural' talent(s), what talent(s) has God equipped you with? (Describe the type of work you do, or skill(s) that you enjoy doing most - What are you passionate about? What do you do best?):

_____   _____

_____   _____

_____   _____

Do you believe in 'Spiritual gifts'? (Heavenly Treasures) _____ Yes _____ No

Have you been blessed with 'Spiritual gifts'? _____ Yes _____ No

If blessed <u>with</u> 'Spiritual gifts' which gifts have you been blessed to receive? [Do not include the "gift of Salvation" or the "gift of the Holy Spirit"].

_____

_____

_____

Are you 'operating' in (or developing) your 'gifts and talents'? _____ Yes_____ No

If 'operating' in your 'gifts and talents,' are you using them to perform any type of Kingdom work/service? (Romans 12:4-8) _____ Yes_____ No

If you <u>have</u> belief in 'Spiritual gifts,' why is it that you <u>do not</u> believe in this particular 'gift of prophecy'? [Explain YOUR predicament]:

_____

_____

_____

_____

What do you have to say about the Lord's "giftings" and "talents" released into the life of the author, revealed through prophecies received? Explain YOUR theory:

_____

_____

_____

_____

❖ **Have you <u>ever</u> been given a Prophecy?** _____ Yes _____ No _____ Not Sure

Has anyone ever come up to you - especially a person you did not know - while at Church, the mall, your work place, on the street, etc. and began speaking things to you concerning:

- Your life's "predicament or circumstance"? _____ Yes _____ No
- Your "gifts" and "talents"? _____ Yes _____ No
- Your "heart's desires"? _____ Yes _____ No
- Things about your future? _____ Yes _____ No

[**Note:** If you answered "**Yes**" to <u>any</u> of the last questions, more than likely, you have been given a prophecy. And if <u>any</u> of these things were present or have come to pass in your life, more than likely, you were given 'true' Prophecy.]

❖ **Although you <u>do not</u> believe in prophecy:**

Would you be willing to listen (have 'ears to hear') if a prophecy was delivered to you in your future? _____ Yes _____ No

If a prophecy was delivered to you in your future, and you received it - accepted what was revealed unto you - would you be "willing to wait on God" (the gatekeeper) for His 'divine' guidance (help) to bring prophecy to pass? _____ Yes _____ No

If <u>willing</u> to wait on God:

And YOUR Prophecy came to pass, would you then believe? (*II Chronicles 20:20*)
_____ Yes _____ No

Reflections of Prophecies Fulfilled:

> If you completed "testimonials": You now have YOUR own 'Reflections' of "Prophecy Fulfilled" - Prophetic (personal) manifestations of 'works of the Lord' in your life.

- ✓ Natural talents are ['innate'] skills we are blessed with at birth.

- ✓ Spiritual gifts are 'blessings' received from the "Holy Spirit" when one becomes borne again.

- ✓ Natural talents combined with spiritual gifts makes one "useful for the Master's good works."

- ✓ All 'Kingdom work' does not consist of work/service directly in a Church [building or home]. Work for the 'Body of Christ' consists of developing and using your gifts and talents to bless God's people in general, being the best that you can be wherever you are.

- ✓ The 'gift of Prophecy' is an "anointing" many people (some Christians as well) believe ended with completion of the 'New Testament'. However, Acts 2:17 & 18 clearly states: *"And it shall come to pass in the last days, saith God, I will pour out of my Spirit upon all flesh: and your sons and your daughters shall prophesy....*

- ✓ Certain tests will confirm the 'gift of prophecy'. Prophecy will: 1) Confirm prior revelations; 2) Reveal gifts and talents; 3) Line up with your hearts desires [what you feel and believe]; 4) Reveal present or past circumstances; 5) Reveal future, and eventually come to pass - manifest.

Chapter Reflections: (Write additional thoughts/feelings about this Chapter here:)

_____

_____

_____

_____

_____

_____

Chapter 13

Dreams Fulfilled

"Fairy tales are fables"... and fables are untruths! So those of you "Wishing upon a Star"... keep wishing! But "Dreams"... as long as you keep dreaming, some "dreams do come true!"

My Reflections:

I believe in 'dreams' of destiny. _____ Yes _____ No

I believe in 'visions' of destiny. _____ Yes _____ No

I believe in angels. _____ Yes _____ No

I have 'dreamed dreams' of destiny. _____ Yes _____ No

I have 'seen visions' of destiny. _____ Yes _____ No

I have had 'prayers' that have been answered. _____ Yes _____ No

I have had 'dreams' and 'visions' come to pass. _____ Yes _____ No

I have experienced 'Spiritual Conception'. _____ Yes _____ No

☐ I have 'Reflections of Dreams Fulfilled'.
☐ I do not have 'Reflections on Dreams Fulfilled'.

> ➤ Complete (1) of (2) Main Sections based on YOUR response to "Dreams Fulfilled."

❖ **I have 'Reflections of Dreams Fulfilled':** ☐

Testimonials

I have 'childhood' [life's] dreams that have been fulfilled. _____ Yes _____ No

I have 'dreams [visions] of destiny' [Promises from God] that have been fulfilled. _____ Yes _____ No

I have 'prayer supplications' that have been answered. _____ Yes _____ No

I have entered the 'Promised Land' (come into 'mutual' promises of God; and things He has 'personally' promised me). _____ Yes _____ No

❖ **When you first saw a 'dream' or 'vision' of destiny:**

Were you aware it was from God? Or did you ignore it, not realizing it could be your future? _____ I was aware of it. _____ I ignored it.

Were you shocked when you realized it was a 'dream' or 'vision' of your destiny (part of God's 'Master' plan for your life)? _____ Yes _____ No

❖ **What do you have to say about these accounts on "Dreams Fulfilled"?**

"The Ideal Mate": (These 'mystical' dreams and detailed revelations that led to the manifestation of "marriage"):

_____

_____

_____

_____

"Writing a Book": (These detailed revelations; 'mystical' "visits from an angel"; hearing the 'spiritual' voices and reports [messages] that led to manifestation of "authorship"):

_____

_____

_____

_____

"Business Ownership": (These detailed revelations that led to manifestation of "self-publishing"):

_____

_____

_____

_____

Can you see the "divine connections" between prophecies received and revelations [prophetic interpretations] of dreams and visions as they relate to manifestation of the "Lord's Blessings" ["Dreams Fulfilled"] in the life of the author? _____ Yes_____ No

What do you have to say <u>overall</u> about "Reflections on The Lord's Blessings" ["Dreams Fulfilled"]?:

_____

_____

_____

_____

❖ **Do you share similar experiences of _'Dreams Fulfilled'_ with the author?**
_____ Yes_____ No

> ➤ DO NOT complete this section if YOUR response was **'No'**

Do you often submit prayer requests [supplications] to God concerning your hearts desires?
_____ Yes_____ No

Express in a few words how you felt after coming into revelation that God loved you enough to release unto your 'hearts desires':

_____

_____

After coming into revelation that your prayer requests, dreams dreamed and/or visions seen could be, and lead to, your purpose and destiny [future]:

Did you take steps (make the sacrifices necessary) towards walking into [fulfilling] your 'purpose and destiny'? _____ Yes_____ No

'Reflect' on an *'Answered Prayer Request'* [Supplication] that concerned your future:

_____

_____

_____

_____

_____

_____

'Reflect' on a **'Dream'** that concerned your future (you believed in what you had seen, or conceived in your spirit) that has manifested in the natural:

_____

_____

_____

_____

_____

_____

'Reflect' on a **'Vision'** that you saw concerning your future (you believed in what you had seen, or conceived in your spirit) that has manifested in the natural:

_____

_____

_____

_____

_____

_____

Did you consider it a 'miracle' when YOUR prayer requests, dreams dreamed and/or visions seen manifested in the natural? (Came to pass/fruition) _____ Yes _____ No

How did you feel after coming into revelation that you could actually become 'all that God has desired (willed) for you to be'? [Just list a few words:]

_____

_____

How did you feel on this 'joyous occasion' of coming into revelation that God was directing your paths - drawing you nearer unto Him simply through a prayer request, dream or vision?

_____

_____

How did you feel after coming into revelation that "God's word does not return unto Him void" - *Isaiah 55:11* (this 'mystery [hidden truth] of the kingdom of heaven' personally unveiled unto you)?

_____

_____

Did you experience any unexpected delays (while waiting for manifestations)?
_____ Yes_____ No

Did you experience any unexpected outcomes? (Manifestations of blessings that surprised you, including those which you were not expecting) _____ Yes_____ No

As dreams descended, did you keep watch for the 'dream snatchers' and 'body snatchers' that passed by? _____ Yes_____ No

Did you share your 'Good News' (manifestations of blessings) with anyone? _____ Yes_____ No

❖ **I _do not_ have 'Reflections on Dreams Fulfilled':** ☐

Do you have any 'childhood' [life's] dreams that have been fulfilled? _____ Yes_____ No

Do you have any 'dreams' [or visions] of purpose and/or destiny [promises from God] waiting to be fulfilled (released) in your life? _____ Yes_____ No

Do you have any 'prayer requests' [supplications] that have been answered?_____ Yes_____ No

Do you believe in "spiritual conception?" (Although born of flesh, the ability to give birth in the natural [physical] to things conceived in the spirit - through a prayer request, prophecy, dream or a vision) _____ Yes_____ No

How do you think you would feel if you came into revelation that "God loved you enough to give you His 'divine guidance' (especially 'messages' sent by an angel) on how to come into the 'desires of your heart'?"

_____

_____

How do you <u>think</u> you would feel if you came into revelation that you could "actually become all that God has desired (willed) for you to be?"

_____

_____

How do you <u>think</u> you would feel if you came into revelation that "God was directing your paths" - drawing you nearer unto Him <u>simply</u> through prayer requests, dreams and visions)?

_____

_____

How do you <u>think</u> you would feel if you came into revelation that "God's word <u>does</u> <u>not</u> return unto Him void" - *Isaiah 55:11* (this 'mystery [hidden truth] of the kingdom of heaven' being personally unveiled unto you)?

_____

_____

❖ **What do you have to say about these accounts on "Dreams Fulfilled"?**

"The Ideal Mate": (These 'mystical' dreams and detailed revelations that led to the manifestation of "marriage"):

_____

_____

_____

_____

"Writing a Book": (These detailed revelations; 'mystical' "visits from an angel"; hearing the 'spiritual' voices and reports [messages] that led to manifestation of "authorship"):

_____

_____

_____

_____

Do you believe it was the 'voice' of an "angel from the Lord" the author heard?
_____ Yes_____ No;

Or, would you describe the author as being "delusional?" _____ Yes_____ No

If you described the author as "delusional":

What do you have to say about manifestations of the book and this workbook you now hold in your hand? Explain your theory:

_____

_____

_____

_____

"Business Ownership": (These detailed revelations that led to manifestation of "self-publishing"):

_____

_____

_____

_____

Can you see the "divine connections" between prophecies received and revelations [prophetic interpretations] of dreams and visions as they relate to manifestations of the "Lord's Blessings" ["Dreams Fulfilled"] in the life of the author? _____ Yes_____ No

What do you have to say <u>overall</u> about "Reflections on The Lord's Blessings" ["Dreams Fulfilled"]:

_____

_____

_____

_____

❖ **Do you share similar experiences of 'Dreams' and/or 'Visions' of Purpose & Destiny with the author?** _____ Yes_____ No

> ➤ DO NOT complete this section if YOUR response was '**No**'

| **Testimonials** |

When you first saw a 'dream or vision': Were you aware that it was from God? Or did you ignore it - not realizing it could be, or lead to, your 'true' life's purpose or destiny [future]?
_____ I was aware of it.   _____ I ignored it.

When you realized it was a 'dream or vision' of purpose or destiny' (God's 'Master' plan for your life) were you shocked? _____ Yes_____ No

Did you share your 'Good News' ('dream or vision') with anyone? _____ Yes_____ No

If you <u>shared</u> your 'dream or vision' of "Purpose & Destiny" with someone, did they receive your 'Good News'(Wish you well)? _____ Yes_____ No

What 'dreams' or 'visions' of Purpose and/or Destiny have you seen? (Briefly describe at least (2) God has revealed concerning His 'will' [desire] for you):

1) _____

_____

2) _____

_____

Do you believe that you are "expecting a miracle"? (The 'impossible' [a complete and perfect work] to manifest in your life) _____ Yes_____ No

Are you looking forward to "Seasons of New Beginnings" springing forth? _____ Yes_____ No

Have you waited long for these dreams/visions to come to pass? _____ Yes_____ No

Have you done the first thing [work] God has asked you to do? (Made any required effort on your part concerning steps towards fulfilling your dream - and His will for you) _____ Yes_____ No

Are you remaining obedient and steadfast in faith? (Walking upright; believing what has been revealed unto you) _____ Yes_____ No

Have you cast down all 'negative' imaginations - your own and those from other individuals (the 'dream snatchers' and 'body snatchers')? _____ Yes_____ No

- Continue to wait patiently for your hearts desires. If God has shown you things (promises) concerning your future (destiny), as long as you remain obedient - do what He tells you to do; and remain steadfast in faith - YOUR 'dreams and visions' seen are destined to come true.

- God may be waiting to release many desires at once. Remember, you are 'worthy' of what He has planned for (promised) you. But you <u>must</u> have faith; which allows ability to conceive in your spirit, things He has predestined for you.

Reflections of Dreams Fulfilled:

> If you completed "testimonials": You now have YOUR own 'Reflections' of "Mysteries [hidden truths] of the Kingdom of Heaven Unveiled"

✓ We are 'spirit' beings living as 'human' beings (a living spirit with a soul, living inside a fleshly body).

Dreams and visions come from the 'spirit' side of man. The intellect of man (the 'human' mind [brain]) functions at a limited capacity; the other functionality comes from the intuitive 'spirit' side of man - the other side of YOUR IQ (intellect).

✓ The Holy Spirit brings 'true' knowledge - the gifts of 'wisdom, knowledge and understanding of revelation' (discernment) to the 'spirit' of man.

✓ Everyone dreams and visualizes - the 'spirit' of man (living soul) never sleeps.

Dreams and visions can become mystical; they can bring meaningful, life-changing events of purpose and destiny to one's life. And, because these dreams and visions can seem so far-fetched at times, people ignore them and/or do not tell anyone about them.

✓ God speaks (ministers) to man through dreams and visions - in the spirit realm (e.g. Job 33:14-18; Isaiah 6; Daniel 2; Acts 10). While awake - in the natural realm - man is usually conscious of only himself (the 'human' side; the flesh) and typically does not see or hear what God may be revealing spiritually, unless one has "eyes to see" and "ears to hear." (Psalm 19:2)

✓ Angels are 'spiritual' beings created to serve God. Those that have not fallen, work for the kingdom of God, in various capacities, in the 'heavenlies' and in this 'earthly' realm. (References of angels are found throughout the Old and New Testaments)

✓ Remember, God's promises to you (your hearts desires) are for His purposes and His Glory in your life. And if you stay the course, they are destined to come true.

"What I tell you in darkness, that speak ye in light: and what you hear in the ear; that preach ye upon the housetops." - Matthew 10:27.

Chapter Reflections: (Write additional thoughts/feelings about this Chapter here:)

_____

_____

_____

_____

_____

Chapter 14

Greener Pastures

Manifestations of prophecies, prayer requests and dreams and visions came into fruition after learning (experiencing) many "life lessons" and passing "countless tests." [In the midst of each "life lesson" an examination (test) of your spirit (heart) is made, and as you pass these tests, "spiritual gifts" imparted become keener].

"Instructions on Life Lessons"

"There is no greater lesson learned, than a lesson taught by the 'Master' (God) Himself." There are many instruction manuals, training manuals and standard operating procedural (SOP) manuals, but none compare to the "Living Word" (Bible) when it comes to training a person the way s/he should go.

My Reflections:

I have learned many "life lessons." _____ Yes_____ No

I have drawn nearer unto God. _____ Yes_____ No

I am (on my way to) living life as God has planned for me to live it. _____ Yes_____ No

I have 'Seasons of New Beginnings' springing forth. _____ Yes_____ No

I have received blessings in 'double portions'. _____ Yes_____ No

The Lord is my Shepherd; I shall not want. (He maketh me to lie down in "Green Pastures")
_____ Yes_____ No

☐ I have 'Reflections of Greener Pastures'.
☐ I <u>do not</u> have 'Reflections on Greener Pastures'.

❖ **I have 'Reflections of Greener Pastures':** ☐

"He maketh me to lie down in green pastures: he leadeth me beside the still waters." - Psalm 23:2.

Testimonials

Are you remaining 'steadfast' in faith? (Believing in the things of God; His 'corporate' [mutual] and 'individual' [personal] promises) _____ Yes _____ No

Do you believe the Lord has been directing your paths to move forward to step out into that which He has called you to? (Can you see the "divine connections"?) _____ Yes _____ No

Since using this 'devotional' workbook, have you learned (come to know) [more] about God? _____ Yes _____ No

Since using this 'devotional' workbook, have you drawn nearer unto God? (Been lead beside the still waters). _____ Yes _____ No

Briefly describe changes that have taken place in your ways of <u>thinking</u> [beliefs] and ways of <u>living</u> [traditions] since entering 'Greener Pastures':

_____

_____

_____

_____

_____

_____

Have you learned to deal with "life-changing" events, including those that are not so harmonious (knowing God is with you and will see you through it)? [Philippians 4:7] _____ Yes _____ No

What do you have to say <u>overall</u> about the reports on "Kingdom Work?" (These detailed, 'chronological accounts' of [future] revelations that have come to pass; and manifestation ("Completion") of this 'devotional' workbook you now hold in your hand):

_____

_____

_____

_____

Do you believe 'these works' ["teaching tools"] were a 'dispensation' from the Lord?
_____ Yes_____ No

Do you believe 'these works' ["teaching tools"] are "a declaration unto the Lord?" (A"Labor of Love") _____ Yes_____ No

Do you think if the author would have ignored these dreams and visions, prophecies received, and heavenly voices heard, the 'heavenly treasures' received would have been released unto her?
_____ Yes_____ No

Do you believe the Lord has been directing the paths of the author? (Can you see the "divine connections"?) _____ Yes_____ No

Do you agree with the author's "Instructions on Life Lessons?" _____ Yes_____ No

Do you know the differences in: a promise; a blessing; and a miracle? _____ Yes_____ No

What do you have to say <u>overall</u> about "Reflections on Greener Pastures?" (These 'Seasons of New Beginnings' springing forth; their revelations and manifestations):

_____

_____

_____

_____

Do you believe the Lord has been directing YOUR paths (Can you see the 'divine connections'?)
_____ Yes_____ No

Do you share similar experiences of *'Greener Pastures'* with the author?...

❖ **Have you ever received blessings in 'double portions'?** _____ Yes_____ No

> ➤ DO NOT complete this section if YOUR response was **'No'**

Briefly describe your 'double portions' of Spiritual blessings (Isaiah 61:7):

1_____

2_____

3_____

Have these 'double portions' poured out unto you changed your way of living? (Are you living a more prosperous life?) _____ Yes_____ No

❖ **Did you take a 'final' exam before moving into "Greener Pastures?"** _____ Yes_____ No

"But he knoweth the way that I take: when he hath tried me, I shall come forth as gold." - Job 23:10.

> ➤ DO NOT complete this section if YOUR response was '**No**'

Did you cry 'tears of joy' and 'tears of pain'? _____ Yes_____ No

Did you experience any heart-breaking, life-changing events? _____ Yes_____ No

Did you encounter 'body snatchers' and 'dream snatchers' along the way? _____ Yes_____ No

Were you lonely at times? (Standing alone, while steadfast in faith, in order to come into things God had planned for you) _____ Yes_____ No

Have you developed "a 'peace' within which passeth all understanding." (*Philippians 4:7*) _____ Yes_____ No

What did your 'final' exam consist of that led you into "Greener Pastures?" (Briefly describe these challenges of faith and things that took place in the 'supernatural' whereby you knew in your spirit, would place you on the road to "Mountain Highs"):

_____

_____

_____

_____

_____

❖ **How deep is YOUR Faith?... See if you <u>can</u> answer this question:**

What does a "believer in the things unseen" [a person of faith] do - after seeing certain things ("mysteries [hidden truths] of the kingdom of Heaven" unveiled?)

Write your response here: _____

_____

_____

[**Note:** There are various levels of faith. If you answered this question, your faith runs deep - you have "seen" <u>and</u> "heard" some things! (Do you have "20/20" Vision?)]

❖ **I *do not* have 'Reflections on Greener Pastures':** ☐

"Give unto them beauty for ashes, the oil of joy for mourning, the garment of praise for the spirit of heaviness; that they might be called trees of righteousness, the planting of the Lord, that he might be glorified." - Isaiah 61:3.

Do you regularly seek [guidance] from the "Holy Spirit?" (John 10:27 & 28) _____ Yes_____ No

Do you believe the Lord has been directing YOUR path to move forward to step into that which He has called you to? (Can you see any "divine connections"?) _____ Yes_____ No

Are you remaining 'steadfast' in faith? (Believing in the things of God; His 'corporate' [mutual] and 'individual' [personal] promises) _____ Yes_____ No

Have you learned to deal with "life-changing" events, including those that are not so harmonious (knowing God is with you and will see you through it)? [Philippians 4:7] _____ Yes_____ No

What do you have to say <u>overall</u> about the reports on "Kingdom Work?" (These detailed, 'chronological accounts' of [future] revelations - that came to pass; including manifestation ("Completion") of this 'devotional' workbook you now hold in your hand):

_____

_____

_____

_____

Do you believe "these works" ("teaching tools") were a "dispensation" from God?
_____ Yes_____ No

Do you believe "these works" ("teaching tools") are a "declaration unto the Lord?" (A "labor of Love") _____ Yes_____ No

Do you think if the author would have ignored the dreams and visions, prophecies received, or heavenly voices heard, 'heavenly treasures' received would have been released unto her?
_____ Yes_____ No

What do you have to say <u>overall</u> about "Reflections on Greener Pastures?" (These 'Seasons of New Beginnings' springing forth; their revelations and manifestations):

_____

_____

_____

_____

Since using this 'devotional' workbook, have you come to know (learned) more about God? _____ Yes_____ No

Since using this 'devotional' workbook, have you drawn nearer unto God? (Been lead beside the still waters). _____ Yes_____ No

Do you know the differences in: a promise; a blessing; and a miracle? _____ Yes_____ No

Do you agree with the author's "Instructions on Life Lessons?" _____ Yes_____ No

❖ **Have you learned from YOUR "Life Lessons?"** _____ Yes _____ No

| Respond to (1) of the (2) sections that apply to you: |

☐ **I have learned from MY "Life Lessons":**

Testimonials

Have you 'figured the factions' of the parts you played in some of your life's predicaments? _____ Yes_____ No

Have you counted YOUR costs (the price you already paid [sacrifices made] to move on into "Greener Pastures")? _____ Yes_____ No

Has the enemy stolen and/or destroyed much? _____ Yes_____ No

Have you taken back what the enemy has stolen? _____ Yes_____ No

Have you rebuilt what the enemy has destroyed? _____ Yes_____ No

Have you been enlightened through the "Spirit of Truth?" (John 14:6) _____ Yes_____ No

❖ **How deep is YOUR Faith?... See if you can answer this question:**

What does a "believer in the things unseen" [a person of faith] do - after seeing certain things ("mysteries [hidden truths] of the kingdom of Heaven" unveiled?)

Write your response here: _____

_____

_____

[**Note:** There are various levels of faith. If you answered this question, your faith runs deep - you have "seen" and "heard" some things! This is a 'Reflection of Greener Pastures': the Lord thy God enlightening you, bringing you into Truth. (You may have "20/20" Vision!)]

List at least (3) "life lessons" you have learned that will (have) put you on your path to "Greener Pastures" or lead (led) you towards "Mountain Highs?" (Describe your 'renewed' mindset):

1. _____
   _____

2. _____
   _____

3. _____
   _____

> If you learned from your "Life Lessons," in this case, the Lord has been directing your paths. YOU DO have "Reflections of Greener Pastures." Praise God! He is so "worthy to be praised!"

☐ **I have *not* learned from MY "Life Lessons":**

Are you still majoring in 'ungodly' disciplines? _____ Yes _____ No

Is the enemy still stealing from you and/or deceiving you? _____ Yes _____ No

Is the enemy still destroying things in your life (dreams, finances, family bonds, personal and social relationships, etc.)? _____ Yes _____ No

Wouldn't you like to take back what the enemy has stolen from you? or, Rebuild what the enemy has destroyed? _____ Yes _____ No

❖ **Besides the price [sacrifices] Jesus paid (for us) upon the cross:**

Have you ever counted YOUR own costs - the price you have already paid [your sacrifices made] through the many 'trials and tribulations' you have overcome? _____ Yes _____ No

Did you know that many of the 'trials and tribulations' you have overcome were paths allowing ability for you to move on into "Greener Pastures"? _____ Yes _____ No

Do you have the ability to accept TRUTH? (John 14:6) _____ Yes _____ No

> If you have not learned from your "Life Lessons": Repent and ask God to "renew your mind" (Romans 12:2-21) and Register for the "class of a lifetime" - "Discipleship 101" (Luke 14:25-33)

"I will instruct thee and teach thee in the way which thou shalt go: I will guide (counsel) thee with mine eye." - Psalm 32:8

Reflections of Greener Pastures:

> If you completed "testimonials": You now have YOUR own 'Reflections' on "Guidance from the bright and morning star" - "Works of the Lord in your life as 'a lamp unto your feet' and a 'light unto your path'." (*Psalm 119:105*)

✓ **Promises** - from God are things He has 'corporately' (as a whole; mutually) or 'individually' (personally) agreed to release into the lives of His children.

✓ **Blessings** - from God bring provision, favor, and increase; they are 'heavenly' treasures of prosperity released into the lives of His children.

At times, God will release 'double portions' of blessings into the lives of His children for humiliation and/or dishonor suffered. (Job 42:10 and Isaiah 61:7)

✓ **Miracles** - from God show miraculous signs and wonders [demonstrations], or a complete and perfect work; they are 'supernatural' works that only God has power to perform released into the lives of His children.

✓ **Faith** - in God is a 'gift' from God. There are processes of [faith] one must go through in order to "grow greater in grace." Following are scriptures on these various levels of faith:

- Gift of faith - Hebrews 11
- Justifying faith - Genesis 15:6
- Doctrinal faith - Jude 3
- Saving faith - Acts 16:31
- Indwelling faith - Galatians 2:20 & Romans 1:17
- Daily faith - 2 Corinthians 5:7

Chapter Reflections: (Write additional thoughts/feelings about this Chapter here:)

_____

_____

_____

_____

_____

_____

Chapter 15

Paths to Righteousness

*H*ealing from "brokenness of past" and "disappointments within," brings with it deliverance - God will redeem your soul; He will make you whole. A renewed heart allows ability to see (visualize) things from a different perspective (in your thinking, your actions, your attitudes, and past traditions).

In "Season of New Beginnings" you will have fresh oil (a new anointing) and a bountiful harvest of fresh fruit (spiritual blessings) for a season long waited to enter into - on your way to "Mountain Highs!"

My Reflections:

I believe in 'everlasting' life (true Salvation - the believers' final destiny). _____ Yes_____ No

I believe in the 'Book of Life' (the book where the names of [believers] are recorded). _____ Yes_____ No

I have a 'new' attitude; a renewed heart - I have been made whole. _____ Yes_____ No

I have 'fresh oil' and 'fresh fruit' on my way to "Mountain Highs." _____ Yes_____ No

The 'Windows of Heaven' have opened up unto me. _____ Yes_____ No

He restoreth my soul: he leadeth me in the "Paths to Righteousness." _____ Yes_____ No

☐ I have 'Reflections of Paths to Righteousness'.

☐ I <u>do not</u> have 'Reflections on Paths to Righteousness'.

❖ **I have 'Reflections of Paths to Righteousness':** ☐

"He restoreth my soul: he leadeth me in the paths of righteousness for his name's sake." - Psalm 23:3.

Testimonials

The Lord has been a 'lamp unto my feet' and 'a light unto my path'. _____ Yes _____ No

I have entered (I am on my way) into the 'fullness' of God's promises. _____ Yes _____ No

I have made many sacrifices, including leaving certain people and certain things behind. _____ Yes _____ No

I am under God's amazing grace; having 'unmerited' favor with my Father. _____ Yes _____ No

I am bearing fruit of righteousness; I have a planting from the Lord. _____ Yes _____ No

I am walking in Victory! I have true Salvation! (I have overcome the world, the flesh, and the enemy). _____ Yes _____ No

What do you have to say about "Additional Prophecies Received?" (These prophetic [future] revelations of changes taking place in the life of the author):

_____

_____

_____

_____

What do you have to say <u>overall</u> about "Reflections on Paths to Righteousness?"

_____

_____

_____

_____

Do you share similar experiences of *"Paths to Righteousness"* with the author?...

❖ **Have 'Windows of Heaven' opened up unto you?**

"And the Lord went before them by day in a pillar of cloud, to lead them the way; and by night in a pillar of fire, to give them light; to go by day and night:" - Exodus 13:21.

Have you come into "A Spiritual Awakening?" (Have things 'previously' unseen been personally unveiled unto you - strengthening YOUR faith in the Lord [God]) _____ Yes_____ No

Have you discovered 'true' Purpose & Destiny? _____ Yes_____ No

Have you received 'bountiful' blessings from Heaven (provision, favor, increase, etc.)? [Malachi 3:10] _____ Yes_____ No

Do you live by the 'law of the Spirit' <u>and</u> not by 'traditions of man'? _____ Yes_____ No

Do you believe what happens on earth is known in heaven? _____ Yes_____ No

❖ **Does your description of God differ now, from your description of Him given in Chapter 3 (*"Time with God"*)?** _____ Yes_____ No

Since using these "teaching tools" (book and workbook), what have you learned [come to know] about God that you <u>did</u> <u>not</u> know about Him? [Can you list (7) things?]:

1. _____
2. _____
3. _____
4. _____
5. _____
6. _____
7. _____

Since using these "teaching tools" (book and workbook) has God seen <u>any</u> change(s) in you? _____ Yes_____ No

If God <u>has</u> seen change(s) in you:

Briefly declare your proclamations describing at least (3) 'positive' life-changes God (and other people) has seen in you? (*"Come and hear, all ye that fear God, and I will declare what he hath done for my soul"* - Psalm 66:16:)

1. _____
2. _____
3. _____

❖ **I _do not_ have 'Reflections on Paths to Righteousness':** ☐

Are you on a 'righteous' path? (In right standing with God) _____ Yes_____ No

Are you proclaiming 'true' Salvation [Deliverance]? (Have you overcome the world, the flesh, and the enemy?) _____ Yes_____ No

Do you trust God to supply of all your needs? _____ Yes_____ No

Do you ever praise (thank) God for things He has done for you? _____ Yes_____ No

Are you living by the 'traditions of man' (ways of the world) and not by 'laws of the Spirit'? (Romans 8:4-6; Colossians 2:8). _____ Yes_____ No

Do you believe what happens on earth is known in heaven? _____ Yes_____ No

Do you know the steps you must take in order to come into God's will for your life? _____ Yes_____ No

Are you willing to become "all that God wants you to be?" _____ Yes_____ No

Have you ever made sacrifice(s) of leaving certain people and/or certain things behind? _____ Yes_____ No

Would you be willing to declare 'works of the Lord' in your life even if things ('specific' works) God has personally planned for you to do in this earthly realm <u>have</u> <u>not</u>, as of yet, been 'personally' revealed unto you? _____ Yes_____ No

What do you have to say about the "Additional Prophecies Received?" (The prophetic [future] revelations and those that have come to pass in the life of the author):

_____

_____

_____

_____

What do you have to say <u>overall</u> about "Reflections on Paths to Righteousness?"

_____

_____

_____

_____

Does your description of God differ now, from your description of Him given in Chapter 3 ("Time with God")? _____ Yes_____ No

Have you come into "A Spiritual Awakening?" (Have things 'previously' unseen been personally unveiled unto you - strengthening YOUR faith in the Lord [God]) _____ Yes_____ No

Since using these "teaching tools" (book and workbook) what have you learned [come to know] about God that you <u>did</u> <u>not</u> know about Him? [See if you can list (7) things]:

1. _____
2. _____
3. _____
4. _____
5. _____
6. _____
7. _____

Since using these "teaching tools" (book and workbook) has God seen <u>any</u> change(s) in you? _____ Yes_____ No

If God <u>has</u> seen change(s) in you:

Briefly declare your proclamations by describing at least (3) 'positive' life-changes God (and other people) has seen in you?

1. _____
2. _____
3. _____

"Come and hear, all ye that fear God, and I will declare what he hath done for my soul." - Psalm 66:16.

If you have learned (more) about God and God has seen 'positive' change(s) in you, in this case, YOU DO <u>have</u> 'Reflections of Paths to Righteousness'- Praise God! He is so "worthy to be praised!"

Reflections of Paths to Righteousness

> If you completed this 'devotional' workbook: You have created a 'spiritual' journal detailing "life-changing" events of "works of the Lord" in your life - YOUR OWN "Reflections of A Spiritual Awakening." YOU have seen God's face! (For the first time, or like never before!)

Author's Workbook Reflections: Testimonials related to workbook's manifestation:

- *Excerpts (3)* taken from the book "Reflections of A Spiritual Awakening":

  (1) [It is my hope some of you reading this book take time out to reflect on some of your dreams and visions (or life's predicaments), when (or where) God may have personally shown Himself to you.] **Chapter 6:** Page 62; 2006.

  (2) But, *manifestation* of "teaching" God's word coming to fruition in the form of a book was certainly unforeseen. **Chapter 13:** Page 181; 2008.

  (3) This book was exclusively written... for readers to become familiar with Him and His ways, so they too, may become receivers of His "gifts and blessings" ["heavenly treasures"]. **Chapter 14: Reflections:** Page 207; 2008. (Page 204 - 2009 Edition)

- *Question* addressed to author from a lady customer (never seen before) whom approached her while working in a friends place of business June 15, 2009:

  "Are you writing a training manual or something to do with teaching?"

- *Immediate Response* from the 'Lord' December 14, 2009 after the author solemnly asked: **"Lord, what can I do to sell the book?"**

  - ❖ It's (*referring to book*) a source for the training manual; to "understand and get to know me."

  - ❖ It's a "teaching tool!" This is how you will teach for the uplifting of the Body of Christ. The book is NOT for everybody!

  - ❖ Create the training manual as I first told you... "You are a teacher!"

  - ❖ Promote the book with the manual - the (2) are (1); they are "teaching tools."

  - ❖ This (*referring to manual*) will get their attention to understand the purpose of the book - to learn "truth"; they will be able to "see me." And once they use the manual as a guide in their own life experiences, they will "seek more of me" for themselves.

  - ❖ You will lead them... This is your calling!

  - ❖ Send the book and manual to large, international Christian churches, organizations and study groups. They don't know you now, but will accept TRUTH!

Your Workbook Reflections

❖ **Since coming into revelation of this workbook's manifestation, what are your thoughts?**

(Does it "renew your mind" concerning: God's will, purpose and destiny for your life; belief in God's promises; prophecy; things unseen?)

_____

_____

_____

❖ **Now that you have embraced the 'seeds of empowerment' (purpose) and 'spiritual wealth' (destiny) of this 'devotional' workbook:**

Express how YOU feel inside since 'reflecting' on [revealing] "works of the Lord" in YOUR life:

_____

_____

_____

❖ **Out of all of YOUR "life lessons" so far, what is the one (1) lesson that has 'humbled' you the most?**

Describe this particular lesson <u>and</u> express in a few words why you felt so humbled by it:

Lesson:_____

_____

_____

Reason for Humility: _____

_____

_____

❖ **Would you recommend these "teaching tools" [book and workbook] to anyone else?**
 _____ Yes_____ No

⇨ NOW GO TO THE NEXT PAGE TO TAKE YOUR "Exam"

"EXAM"

~ Reflections of A Spiritual Awakening ~

[Keep in mind: "You must have studied, to show thyself approved" - *II Timothy 2:15*.]

1. Has YOUR 'devotional' workbook reached its ***purpose*** and ***destiny***?

   a) Have you learned (more) truth? (Concerning things of God, Salvation, and how to live a 'true' Christian life) _____ Yes_____ No

   b) Have (additional) "seeds of empowerment" been sown into your life? (Do you feel more 'victorious' in your spiritual walk?) _____ Yes_____ No

   c) Do YOU feel (more) prosperous? (Spiritually healthy and wealthy inside) _____ Yes_____ No

2. Have you come into "A Spiritual Awakening?" _____ Yes_____ No

3. Are YOU prepared for 'eternity'- YOUR 'final' destination?...

   a) Who might YOUR real father be?

   b) Do YOU have 'treasures' stored in heaven?...
      or, Would YOU be counted as one of the sheep for the slaughter?

   c) Are YOU fully persuaded a place has been prepared for YOU... in the "Kingdom of Heaven" that is?

4. In the "End Time" - will YOUR time with God really matter... at the time that matters most to Him?

5. If YOU were 'standing in judgment' at this very moment:

   Would YOUR name be written in the "Lambs book of life" along with other 'true' believers? [People of faith saved by God's grace, and <u>not</u> according to their works (*Ephesians 2:8; II Timothy 1:8 & 9; Philippians 4:3; Revelation 21:27*).]

Aren't you glad this 'exam' was not an "end-time" exam? I know these questions [this 'exam'] seemed scary. But wouldn't it be even scarier if YOUR name not was there... in the "Lambs book of life"... but recorded in 'the other book' where people are 'judged according to their works' (*Revelations 17:8 and 20:12-15*).